Perfect Patisserie

...

Dr. Tim Kinnaird

Perfect Patisserie

Mastering Macarons, Madeleines and More

• • •

FIREFLY BOOKS

A FIREFLY BOOK

Published by Firefly Books Ltd. 2013

First printing

Library and Archives Canada Cataloguing in Publication

Kinnaird, Tim, author
      Perfect patisserie : mastering macarons, madeleines and more / Tim Kinnaird, Keiko Oikawa.
Includes index.
ISBN 978-1-77085-211-2
        1. Pastry. I. Kinnaird, Tim, author II. Title.
TX773.K56 2013   641.86′5   C2013-901832-8

Publisher Cataloging-in-Publication Data (U.S.)

Kinnaird, Tim.
    Perfect patisserie : mastering macarons, madeleines and more / Tim Kinnaird ; photographs by Keiko Oikawa.
160 p. : 24 x 22 cm.
Includes index.
ISBN-13: 978-1-77085-211-2
1. Pastry. 2. Macarons. I. Kinnaird, Tim. II Title.
641.865 dc23   TX773.K5664 2013

Published in the United States by
Firefly Books (U.S.) Inc.
P.O. Box 1338, Ellicott Station
Buffalo, New York 14205

Published in Canada by
Firefly Books Ltd.
50 Staples Avenue, Unit 1
Richmond Hill, Ontario L4B 0A7

Cover design: Erin R. Holmes

Printed in China

Conceived, designed and produced by
Quintet Publishing
The Old Brewery
6 Blundell Street
London
N7 9BH

For Quintet Publishing:
Project editor: Margaret Swinson
Designer: Sophie Martin
Photographer: Keiko Oikawa, Adrian Lawrence
Art director: Michael Charles
Managing editor: Emma Bastow
Publisher: Mark Searle

... CONTENTS

...FOREWORD

This is my second book. The first was a textbook of pediatrics and writing this book has brought into sharp focus just how much my working life has changed. My career change was sparked by a short conversation with Craig, a cameraman filming the 2010 MasterChef TV series in which I took part. Chatting in the pastry kitchen of a 3 Michelin-starred French restaurant, he questioned my plan of opening a restaurant. "Why don't you just stick to pastry?" he asked, "It's what you enjoy most." From that point I decided to pursue my perfect job, making and selling cakes.

I started this second career at my kitchen table. As the business has grown, I've put together a team and gradually recreated a sense of collective achievement that I missed from my days as a doctor. This book was written at the same time I finished planning and opened the first Macarons & More shop in Norwich. To have both projects realized at the same time was incredible. Both the shop and this book owe a large part to the team of gifted and dedicated staff who work with me.

Cooking is healing. More than anything, getting lost in a recipe is one of the experiences I return to during life's ups and downs. Understanding and anticipating how components of a cake come together and build into something delicious relaxes, calms and soothes me.

Although the fussiness and fiddle of pastry making appeals to the pedantic science nerd in me, the world of patisserie shouldn't be seen as complex. The impression that rigid process and rules are everything is an illusion perpetuated by uptight, grumpy pastry chefs. I believe that patisserie is no more complex or difficult than any other type of cookery. It is more about becoming familiar and confident with methods that are perhaps less intuitive. I thoroughly enjoyed writing this book. As well as forcing me to finally write some of my recipes down, it will serve as a memento of an extraordinary time in my life.

Tim

INTRODUCTION

At its simplest, patisserie is about building blocks of texture, flavor and decoration. The components are often easily created, but when assembled into a finished cake they give the illusion of overall complexity. This book provides the ambitious home cook with those tried and tested component recipes, and those of the cakes that highlight them, as well as an understanding of the key techniques behind each component.

The book also includes details of key kitchen equipment and ingredients, and where necessary each chapter covers common patisserie problems and how to avoid them, all of which will give cooks a firm foundation for baking sensational patisserie.

There are some key patisserie cake-making techniques: macaron shells, choux pastry, sweet tart cases, chocolate ganaches, genoise sponge, crème pâtissière and sugarwork decorations. Perfect these skills and your cake world will fall into place; combine and adapt them and an infinite universe of sweet treats will open up.

The principles applied in a professional bakery or pastry kitchen hold true for home baking: precise and immaculate patisserie is the end point of perfected technique, high-quality ingredients and the right recipe. However, it also requires a meticulous approach to all aspects of baking and constructing the cakes.

Planning your patisserie, particularly a new recipe, is key. Spontaneity and inspiration have their place, but carefully thinking through the stages of a recipe and decoration will make a big difference. Working in a clean and ordered kitchen will also reflect in the final cake. Cleaning your work surfaces and tidying and washing up as you go allows you to approach each step of the recipe with a clear head. Pause, take your time and plan what comes next — it's the most important lesson to learn and it will underpin all the technique and detail that follows.

Alongside practicing and refining technique, the joy and challenge of patisserie is the development of your own intuitive cookery skills. Decisions about texture, temperature, taste and appearance are the indefinable differences between good and exceptional cakes. The recipes and guidance in this book should be used as a launch pad for your own journey. Your ingredients, equipment, kitchen temperature and humidity will vary and necessitate minor changes to the recipes and methods.

There will be small differences in outcome for every cake you bake. Some will be better than others, and occasionally a component of the cake will fail. Sometimes a step will need to be repeated, but often it's worth continuing. With a slight change in how the cake is finished or presented, small problems can be magically hidden with a dusting of confectioners' sugar or a covering of fresh cream; next time the problem can be corrected.

Keep notes and learn to trust your instincts.

INGREDIENTS

Much of the finest patisserie is simple. The perfect madeleine has just six ingredients, so the final taste and texture of the cake will rely primarily on the quality of these ingredients. Fresh eggs from organically reared hens and a high fat percentage butter will make a better cake.

••• EGGS

Eggs are undoubtedly the most important and versatile patisserie ingredient. The quality and origin of the eggs used will make a significant difference to your final cakes. Chickens reared with access to grass will lay eggs with a brighter, orange-colored yolk, which will come through in sponges, custards and other patisserie components rich in egg yolk. As well as appearance there are also nutritional benefits, with suggested higher levels of omega fatty acids and vitamins. So alongside the moral imperative to use these eggs, they will bake you a better cake.

FRESH EGGS

From the moment an egg is laid, the characteristics of the egg yolk and white start to change. The egg white becomes more alkaline and this causes it to become thinner and runnier. A more liquefied consistency aids whisking of the egg white, therefore slightly older eggs are preferable to freshly laid eggs when making meringues and foams. However, when separating eggs it's better to use fresh eggs as the white and yolk have more substance and are easier to handle.

As well as the alteration in alkalinity over time, moisture is lost through the porous shells causing the air cell in the egg to increase in size. The amount of air in the egg will determine how buoyant the egg is. As a test, a freshly laid egg will sink to the bottom of a bowl of water; an older egg may float midway between the surface and the bottom; and eggs that float to the surface are likely to be spoiled and should be thrown away.

CRACKING EGGS

Cracking eggs is perhaps the most regularly performed baking technique. Most cooks crack the egg on the side of a bowl. Don't! This technique forces cracked bits of shell into the egg and is much more likely to puncture the yolk beneath. A better way is to confidently tap the side of the egg on the work surface. The two halves of egg shell can then be gently pried apart with the thumbs of both hands.

If small bits of shell do get into the egg, they can be removed by scooping them out with half an egg shell. These little pieces of shell will adhere much better to that than to your fingers.

SEPARATING EGGS

There is equipment available for separating eggs, but you don't need it. The best way of separating an egg white from the yolk is to crack a whole egg into your hand with your fingers partly splayed. This allows the white to run into a bowl below and the yolk to remain in your palm. If small amounts of egg yolk do get mixed in with the white, don't despair. Using the same technique as for fishing out pieces of shell, these bits of yolk may be retrieved with half an egg shell. If a lot of yolk gets mixed in, make an omlet and start again.

Chicken egg sizes

A guide to international sizes and weights

SIZE	MASS
	TRADITIONAL
Size 0	> 2.7 oz (> 77 g)
Size 1	2.5 oz – 2.7 oz (70 g – 77 g)
Size 2	2.3 oz – 2.5 oz (65 g – 70 g)
Size 3	2.1 oz – 2.3 oz (60 g – 65 g)
Size 4	1.9 oz – 2.1 oz (55 g – 60 g)
Size 5	1.8 oz – 1.9 oz (50 g – 55 g)
Size 6	1.6 oz – 1.8 oz (45 g – 50 g)
Size 7	<1.6 oz (< 45 g)

SIZE	MASS			
	USA	CANADA	AUSTRALIA	EUROPE
King size	–	–	2.5 oz – 2.8 oz (71 g – 79 g)	–
Jumbo	> 2.5 oz (71 g)	2.5 oz or more (71 g or more)	2.4 oz – 2.5 oz (67 g – 70 g)	–
Very Large or Extra-Large (XL)	> 2.25 oz (64 g)	2.2 oz – 2.4 oz (62 g – 69 g)	2.1 oz – 2.3 oz (58 g – 67 g)	2.6 oz and over (73 g and over)
Large (L)	> 2 oz (57 g)	1.9 oz – 2.2 oz (56 g – 62 g)	1.8 oz – 2.1 oz (50 g – 60 g)	2.2 oz – 2.6 oz (62 g – 73 g)
Medium (M)	> 1.75 oz (50 g)	1.7 oz – 1.9 oz (49 g – 55 g)	1.5 oz – 1.8 oz (43 g – 50 g)	1.9 oz – 2.2 oz (55 g – 63 g)
Small (S)	> 1.5 oz (43 g)	1.5 oz – 1.7 oz (42 g – 48 g)	–	1.9 oz and under (55 g and under)
Peewee	> 1.25 oz (35 g)	<1.4 oz (41 g)	–	–

PASTEURIZED EGG WHITE AND YOLK

Patisserie tends to require more egg white than egg yolk and this can lead to a glut of unwanted egg yolk in your refrigerator. Small cartons of pasteurized free range egg white are available and can help solve this problem. However, pasteurizing eggs affects their consistency, with the egg white becoming thin and not whisking as well. Look for products that have a small amount of guar gum added, a thickener extracted from the guar bean.

WEIGHING EGGS

Some of the recipes that follow include quantities of egg given in ounces rather than whole egg equivalents. Even within the same egg grade there is a difference in egg weight; similarly, the proportion of egg yolk to egg white in an individual egg varies. Weighing your eggs is more accurate and an important patisserie technique to embrace.

••• FLOUR

Wheat flour supports the architecture of cakes, cookies and pastry. Understanding what flour is and how it works can be helpful when solving baking problems, or if you wish to refine a recipe to your own liking.

Wheat flour is graded on the basis of protein and ash content. The ash content refers to the amount of ash produced after a fixed amount of flour is heated to a high temperature. It correlates to the mineral content of the flour and enables millers to compare and standardize flours.

Of greater significance to home bakers is the protein content, which directly relates to gluten development in the batter or pastry. Convention would suggest that for most patisserie work a flour with a protein content of 9–11 percent (UK plain flour) is best as this level of gluten will allow the structure of the cake to develop but not adversely affect the texture. Flours with a higher protein content may make cakes chewier and denser and are generally reserved for bread making.

However, for some recipes and techniques a higher protein content is helpful. Choux pastry in particular benefits from a higher protein content flour (see page 38), while using a higher protein content flour in cookies creates a chewier cookie.

Unfortunately, the grading of flours in the US, UK and Europe is different. Unless otherwise stated, the recipes in the book refer to UK Plain Flour (protein content 9–11 percent), but have been tested and work for US All Purpose (protein content 8–9 percent).

••• FRUIT

If a cake requires fresh fruit, use fruit that is in season and abundant. This is particularly important with soft fruit and berries: make your favorite strawberry tart when fresh strawberries are in season — it will taste better. High-quality natural fruit extracts and fruit purées are often a better choice for out-of-season fruits.

••• CHOCOLATE

There is a wide range of chocolate available to home cooks, but don't just use cocoa solid percentage as a guide to flavor and quality. We are familiar with regional and geographical variations in tea, coffee and wine, but the same is true for the cocoa bean. A good way of exploring this is to take a relatively simple recipe such as a chocolate tart and try filling it with different regional chocolates. As an example, compare a fruity and spice-flavored Tanzanie chocolate with the full-bodied and bitter Kumabo chocolate (see Resources, page 156).

••• COLORINGS

Natural colorings are a better choice for patisserie components such as macaron shells, frostings and fillings. They are a little more difficult to source but give a much more wholesome and appetizing appearance.

EQUIPMENT

For information on where to source equipment, see the Resources section (page 156).

{1}   HANDS

While machines make light work of mixing and combining ingredients, they are no substitute for your own hands, particularly when judging the correct consistency of combined ingredients. It's much easier to remember the feel of a correctly mixed macaron batter than to recognize it in the bottom of a mixer. Similarly, the feel of egg white as it is whisked by hand is a more accurate way to determine whether it's at soft or stiff peaks. When working with smaller quantities, your hands are often the only option when mixing ingredients together.

{2}   SPATULA

Useful as an all-purpose tool to mix and combine ingredients, but particularly good for folding ingredients together. A flexible thin spatula is best and will allow the incorporation of meringues and whisked egg whites while keeping air and volume in the mix.

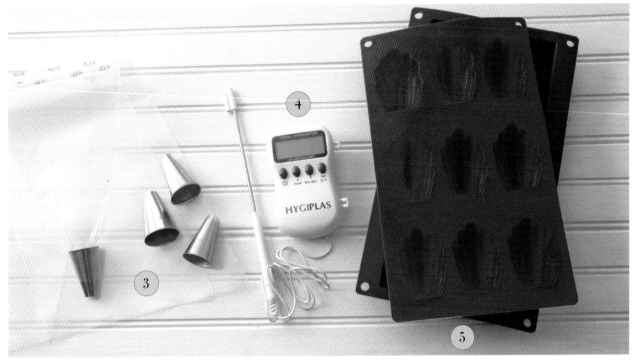

{3} DISPOSABLE PIPING BAGS

Piping bags are essential pieces of patisserie equipment. Disposable bags are readily available in kitchenware and cake-decorating shops, and are preferable to reusable bags, which are difficult to clean and can only be cut to fit one size of piping nozzle.

For small quantities of frostings, fillings and other decorations, a piping bag can be made from a triangular piece of silicone paper or parchment paper.

{4} THERMOMETER

A huge variety of thermometers are available. Instant-read digital thermometers that clip to the side of a pot are best when heating sugar syrups, while non-contact infrared thermometers are useful for chocolate work, enabling quick measurements with no mess.

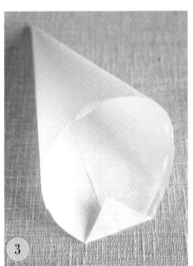

Silicone Molds

Demarle is a great source for these and ships to many countries. Visit www.demarle.com for products and details.

{5} SILICONE MATS AND MOLDS

Flexible silicone mats and molds have revolutionized patisserie. Easy to clean and easy to use, the vast array of molds available allow cakes to be shaped into classic and more unusual designs.

Silicone mats offer the home cook the ability to bake cakes and patisserie components in ways that would be difficult on traditional baking sheets or trays where they may stick. They also allow shorter baking times, which keeps cakes moist and beautifully textured. If you ever have difficulty removing macaron shells from parchment paper, try using a silicone mat instead.

{6} FLEXIBLE PLASTIC BOWL SCRAPER

The bowl scraper is one of the finest kitchen tools ever invented. It's the perfect tool for emptying a bowl of batter or dough, folding and mixing ingredients together, and transferring mixes into piping bags cleanly and efficiently. Used regularly it will significantly improve the accuracy and consistency of your patisserie work, adding another level of control to combining and transferring ingredients. The French Model Scraper is the best of the best and often cheapest.

{7} SCALES

Ideally, you will need two sets of scales. An everyday set of scales that measures in increments of 0.05 oz (1.5 g) is an essential. You need a set that will tare or zero with the container you're weighing into.

A second super-accurate set measuring in increments of 0.005 oz (0.15 g) or even smaller increments will enable you to utilize some of the molecular gastronomy techniques applicable to patisserie. Liquid spherification, modern gelling, thickening and setting agents all need to be measured in precise, tiny amounts.

{8}   FREE-STANDING MIXER

A trusted kitchen friend, mixers not only take the hard work out of patisserie but let you concentrate on the detail of a recipe. For example, making a perfect Italian meringue isn't dependent on how well you can whisk eggs (let the mixer do that), it's about ensuring your sugar syrup is at the right temperature and how evenly you pour it onto the egg white.

Free-standing mixers are also able to mix batters to a degree that's almost impossible to achieve by hand. Batters and mixes relying on eggs alone for their rise need lots of air beating in and a mixer does a much better job.

{9}   OVEN

Love and understand your own oven. Specialist bakery and patisserie ovens offering minute control of temperature and humidity are expensive, huge and necessitate rewiring your home, so appreciate and work with what you know.

Using an oven thermometer, record how the controls of your oven reflect its true temperature. Notice the hot and cold spots: why is it that the macarons on the back right of the tray always brown more than the others? So rotate the tray halfway through baking. Oven humidity can be rapidly reduced by opening the oven door, and increased by heating an empty tray in the bottom of the oven and pouring in hot water at the start of your baking.

Using the oven timer or buying a stand-alone digital timer for accuracy will also make a big difference to your baking success. Keep notes of temperatures and timings for what worked well.

{10} FREEZER

The freezer will become your best friend in the delicate world of patisserie. Most cakes are better stored in the freezer than the refrigerator, as they keep their structure and moisture. However, it's important to wrap them in plastic wrap or seal them in a box to prevent them coming into direct contact with ice.

As well as storing whole cakes, freezers are a great way of storing components made in advance of finishing and serving a cake. Choux pastry (baked and unbaked), genoise sponge and macaron shells will all sit happily in the freezer for a month until needed. Some components even taste better for being frozen and defrosted.

... MACARONS

Macarons are the supermodels of the cake world. At their best, elegant and indefinable delights; at their worst, temperamental divas. However, once you understand how to keep them on the straight and narrow, you will consistently produce a cake that has helped to revolutionize modern patisserie.

With confidence and practice, macaron shell batter may be piped into different shapes and sizes, and adapted to create a range of cakes and desserts. Elongated macalongs work brilliantly as a larger cake or as the basis of a dessert. Larger round shells work wonderfully well with scoops of ice cream or fresh fruit. Delicately colored pink macaron batter can be piped into small heart shapes for Valentine's Day gifts, while larger sheets of baked batter can be used in layered cakes and gâteaux to provide a chewy and crunchy texture.

MACARON SHELLS

The most important component of the macaron shell recipe is the meringue. A perfect meringue leads to a perfect macaron: a crisp, eggshell-like exterior and a moist interior seamlessly blended with a well-defined, flavorful filling.

● ● ● TYPES OF MERINGUE

FRENCH MERINGUE
Egg white and room-temperature sugar whisked together and baked before eating. Used in classics such as pavlovas.

ITALIAN MERINGUE
Egg white whisked with a hot sugar syrup. As the egg white is cooked by the heat in the sugar it may be eaten immediately. If baked it produces a softer, closer textured meringue.

SWISS MERINGUE
Egg white and sugar heated together in a bain-marie to 120°F (50°C) then whisked and baked. This produces a very dense and stable meringue that is often used in sculpting decorations such as meringue mushrooms for the classic Bûche de Noël.

● ● ● AGING EGG WHITES

Aging egg whites affects their consistency and consequently their ability to be whisked. Water evaporates from egg whites and the structure of the proteins in the whites is altered, making them quicker to whisk up and giving a meringue with a consistent texture.

To age whites, the eggs should be separated 1 or 2 days in advance and the whites placed in a bowl in the refrigerator covered in plastic wrap. The wrap should have small holes punctured in it.

Although aging egg whites can be helpful it is not essential for successful macarons. Pasteurized egg white is available in most supermarkets and offers equivalent results. Using freshly separated egg whites is fine, but the eggs used should be at room temperature and the final batter may require additional mixing to create the correct texture before piping.

MACARON FILLINGS

Macaron shells can be sandwiched together with a wide variety
of flavored and textured fillings. Here are the four basic types of filling
with which to start.

••• TYPES OF FILLING

CHOCOLATE GANACHE
A chocolate ganache is a great way of packing flavor
into a macaron. A well-balanced ganache is a brilliant
textural contrast to the crisp macaron shells.

In particular, a white chocolate ganache can be
modified to create a wide range of flavored fillings.
The cream in the ganache may be infused with
different flavors before emulsifying with the white
chocolate. Classic flavors such as vanilla and fruit
purées may be incorporated this way, or more
unusual flavors such as matcha green tea and
melted Christmas candy canes.

BUTTERCREAM
A mix of equal quantities of unsalted butter and
sifted confectioners' sugar beaten together until
smooth produces a versatile and simple filling.
The buttercream can be flavored with fruit essences
or flavorings.

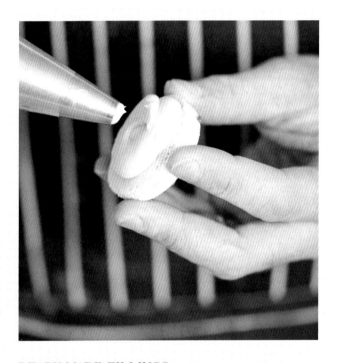

GELS
Modern gelling agents such as gelatin, agar-agar
and carrageenan have enabled new combinations
of flavor and texture. Small cubes of jello pressed
into a ganache or buttercream filling work well,
while liqueurs and spirits may be used to fill
shells if thickened first with xanthan gum.

READY-MADE FILLINGS
Off-the-shelf staples such as jellies and spreads
work well. High-quality fruit preserves can be used
to create delicious fruit macarons, or try filling
shells with jelly and peanut butter to satisfy those
PBJ cravings. Chocolate and nut spreads also work
brilliantly as an alternative to chocolate ganaches.

How to Make
BASIC MACARON SHELLS

There are three methods of making macaron shells (see page 20). French, Italian or Swiss meringue is combined with ground almonds and confectioners' sugar. Baking macarons can be a frustrating process, and using this technique offers a consistent method of preparing them.

Ingredients

7 oz (200 g) confectioners' sugar

7 oz (200 g) ground almonds

5 oz (150 g) egg white (divided into 2 x 2½ oz (75 g) quantities)

7 oz (200 g) superfine sugar

⅕ cup (50 ml) water

coloring paste, if required

Tools

Large copper or stainless steel mixer bowl for egg whites

Large mixer bowl

Small pot

Confectioner's thermometer

Piping bag with ½-inch plain nozzle

Baking sheet

Silicone parchment paper

Template of 1½-inch circles

Method

Step 1

Combine the confectioners' sugar, ground almonds, the first quantity of egg white and beat until well combined. Food coloring can also be added if desired.

Step 2

Place the second quantity of egg white in the bowl of a free-standing mixer or bowl resting on a damp cloth to hold it securely.

Mix the superfine sugar and water together in a small pot. The volume of the sugar and water combined needs to fill the pot at least a quarter full. If the pot is too large the temperature of the syrup will rise too quickly. The syrup is heated to 242°F (117°C) and this requires a good depth of syrup for a thermometer to accurately measure. If you don't have a pot small enough, double or triple the sugar and water quantities then use only half or a third of the final syrup.

As the temperature of the syrup gets close to 242°F (117°C), the egg whites should be whisked until a little frothy. While continuing to whisk, the sugar syrup should be poured onto the egg white. Continue to whisk until stiff peaks form.

Step 3

Preheat the oven to 300°F (150°C). Add the mix from step 1 into the Italian meringue. Beat together slowly for 30 seconds then scrape down the sides of the bowl with a spatula and beat again for a further 30 seconds.

The consistency of the mix at this stage is the most important factor in successful macaron shell baking. The batter needs to flow smoothly and when dropped back into the bowl should spread back into a flat, even surface.

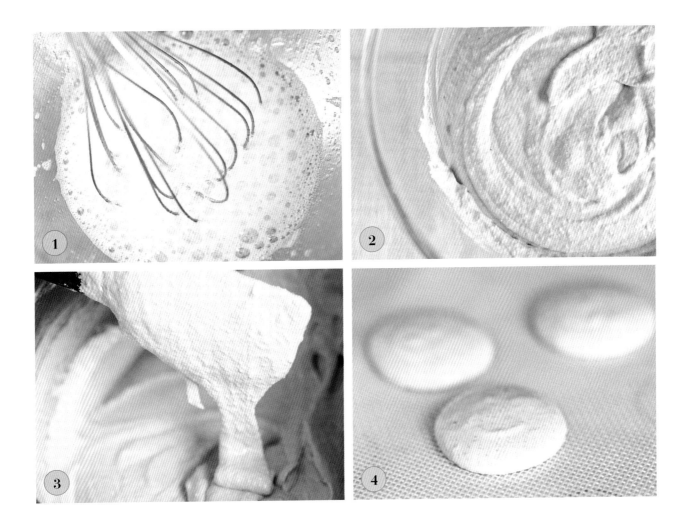

Step 4

Transfer the batter into a piping bag with a ½-inch (1 cm) plain round nozzle. Pipe small rounds of batter onto a baking sheet lined with silicone parchment paper. Using a template of 1½-inch (4 cm) diameter circles approximately 1 inch (2.5 cm) apart will produce a consistent-sized macaron.

Hold the nozzle ½ inch (1 cm) above the surface of the silicone paper. Pipe the batter until it almost fills the circular template. It will continue to spread out after piping. The tip of the nozzle should be swirled off by moving it around the edge of the piped shell; this will help the batter to flow into an even, flat surface.

If the batter is under-mixed, tapping the tray of piped macaron shells will help the batter spread.

Step 5

Most macaron recipes recommend that piped shells are left for a period of time to allow a skin to form before baking. This is a rather inconsistent method as how well a skin forms is dependent on the kitchen's temperature and humidity. A better technique is to place the trays immediately in the preheated oven but reduce the temperature to 32°F (0°C) and bake for 10 minutes. Then turn the heat back up to 300°F (150°C) for 8 to 10 minutes. The macarons are baked when they have a smooth, dry top and have firmed up. They don't need to be completely dry and stiff as they will continue to cook for a few minutes after.

Remove the parchment paper and macarons from the baking tray, allowing the shells to cool on the work surface. This is important as if left on the baking tray the residual heat in the tray will over-cook the shells. Peel the shells from the parchment and pair up.

CRÈME BRÛLÉE MACARONS

The crisp macaron shell acts as the burned caramel crust in this classic-French-dessert-meets-classic-French-cake combination.

Ingredients

1 quantity of macaron shells
   (see page 22)
light brown soft sugar,
   for sprinkling
3½ oz (100 g) egg yolk
2½ oz (75 g) light brown
   sugar
2 vanilla pods
1½ cups (375 ml) heavy
   cream

Method

1. Make the macaron shells as described. Prior to baking, sprinkle or sift a small amount of brown sugar onto each shell.

2. Mix the egg yolks and sugar together in a bowl until smooth. Preheat the oven to 350°F (180°C).

3. Split the vanilla pods and scrape out the seeds. Place the seeds, pods and cream into a small pot and warm until just below boiling point. Retrieve the vanilla pods then pour the hot vanilla-infused cream onto the eggs and sugar. Return this to a clean pot and warm until it thickens.

4. Pour the vanilla custard into a shallow ovenproof dish or bowl and bake in the oven for 15 minutes. A dark brown crust needs to form on the surface of the custard.

5. Remove from the oven and tip the mix into a food processor. The mix at this stage will appear split and ruined — it isn't, have faith and blend it. It will come together as a smooth paste. Chill the mix in the refrigerator until firm enough to pipe.

6. Using a piping bag and a ½-inch (1 cm) plain round nozzle, generously fill a macaron shell with the brûlée mix and top with a second shell. Store in the refrigerator but serve at room temperature. For a bit of drama and additional brûlée taste, blow torch the macaron shell briefly before serving until the brown sugar caramelizes.

JASMINE TEA MACARONS

Infusing different tea flavors into cakes is a fabulous way of adding refined elegance. The finely chopped tea baked into the shell adds a lovely texture and aftertaste.

Ingredients

1 quantity of macaron shells (see page 22)

2 tbsp (30 g) Jasmine tea leaves, finely chopped, to decorate the shells

2 tbsp (30 g) Jasmine tea leaves

½ cup (125 ml) heavy cream

10 oz (275 g) white chocolate, finely chopped

2 oz (60 g) butter, at room temperature

Method

1. Make the macaron shells as described. After piping and before baking, sprinkle the shells with the finely chopped tea.

2. Warm the second quantity of Jasmine tea leaves and cream in a small pot. Heat until almost boiling then set aside and allow the tea to infuse for 5 minutes.

3. Re-heat the cream almost to boiling. Remove the tea leaves by pouring through a sieve onto the chocolate. Stir the chocolate and cream until all the chocolate has melted. If any lumps of chocolate remain, blend the mix with a hand-held blender. Mix the butter into the ganache with a whisk or hand-held blender.

4. Fit a piping bag with a ½-inch (1 cm) plain round nozzle and use to generously fill the macarons with Jasmine tea chocolate ganache. Store in the refrigerator but serve at room temperature.

MAPLE SYRUP, BACON AND BLUEBERRY MACARONS

Here are the classic breakfast flavors combined in a single macaron. The whole blueberry hidden at the center of the macaron elevates and lightens it, providing a burst of fresh flavor. Don't be put off by the use of bacon here. Baking with bacon works fabulously, the saltiness cutting through the sweetness of the maple syrup. It works in the same way as salt with caramel or chocolate.

Ingredients

1 quantity of macaron shells
   (see page 22)
10 slices unsmoked bacon
4 oz (125 g) whole eggs
$^3/_4$ cup (180 ml) maple syrup
7 oz (200 g) unsalted butter,
   chopped and softened
30 plump blueberries

Method

1. Place the strips of bacon on a baking sheet lined with foil. Bake at 250°F (120°C) for 30 to 45 minutes. Exactly how long it takes will depend on how the bacon was prepared and cut; you need bacon that has had almost all of the fat rendered out of it. Remove from the oven and dry on paper towels. The bacon should be brittle and a rich dark brown color. If it isn't, return to the oven for a further 10 to 15 minutes. Place the bacon in a food processor or preferably a spice grinder and blitz until you have smal pieces of bacon.

2. Make the macaron shells as described. After piping and before baking, sprinkle the unbaked shells with the bacon pieces.

3. Lightly whisk the egg yolks in the bowl of a free-standing mixer until just frothy. Place the maple syrup in a small pot and warm to 244°F (118°C). Watch this carefully as the temperature will rise quickly towards the end of heating. Start the egg yolks whisking again and pour in the maple syrup in a thin stream. Continue to whisk the yolks and syrup until thickened and pale in color. Make sure the butter is very soft and an equivalent consistency to the egg and syrup mix, then gradually whisk the butter into the egg mixture.

4. Place the maple buttercream in a piping bag fitted with a ½-inch (1 cm) plain round nozzle. Pipe a generous amount of buttercream onto one shell and push a blueberry into the center of the filling. Place a second shell on top. Store in the refrigerator but serve at room temperature.

CHOCOLATE ORANGE MACALONGS

It's a macaron . . . but longer. These shells work brilliantly as the basis of a more substantial cake or dessert, and lend themselves to a generous filling of berries, chocolate ganaches or even ice cream.

Ingredients

1 quantity of macaron shells
    (see page 22), colored
    orange and made to the
    dimensions in Step 1
¾ cup (180 ml) heavy cream
zest of 3 oranges
9 oz (250 g) milk chocolate,
    finely chopped
2½ oz (75 g) butter, softened
1 tbsp (5 g) cocoa powder,
    for dusting

Method

1. Make the macaron shells as described, adding a small amount of orange coloring. The amount required will depend on the coloring used and the effect you wish to achieve. Macalongs may be piped using a template of 1 x 4-inch (2.5 x 10 cm) oblongs, each 1 inch (2.5 cm) apart from its neighbor to allow for spreading. Fit a piping bag with a ½-inch (1 cm) plain round nozzle and pipe smooth lines of batter to fill the template. Using a small sieve, dust with the cocoa powder. Bake the shells as described in the main recipe.

2. Heat the cream and orange zest in a small pot until almost boiling. Pour the cream over the milk chocolate and stir until all the chocolate has melted. Stick blend the mix if any lumps of chocolate remain. Allow the ganache to cool a little then mix in the softened butter. Allow to cool until stiff enough to pipe.

3. Fit a piping bag with a ½-inch (1 cm) fluted nozzle and use to generously fill the macalongs with the chocolate ganache. Starting at one end of a shell, pipe in a spiral motion along the length of the shell. Macalongs look their best if the top shell is angled slightly, revealing more of the filling. Store in the refrigerator but serve at room temperature.

Macarons

DECORATING MACARON SHELLS

Macaron shells may be decorated before or after baking. Before baking a range of decorative and textural ingredients can be sprinkled over piped shells. Edible lusters and glitters work well. Finely chopped nuts and cocoa powder can also be used, but do so sparingly. Over-decorating before baking can create problems with the baking of the shells, causing cracked shells.

••• WHAT YOU WILL NEED

Ingredients

Food coloring

Isopropyl alcohol

Tools

Small pots for mixing

Round-tip and flat-edge paint brushes suitable for food

STORING AND SERVING MACARONS

After filling, macarons need time to mature. To create the perfect texture the filling needs time to blend and slightly soften the shell. This is best achieved by storing the macarons in a refrigerator for 24 hours. Macarons also store well in the freezer for up to 6 weeks.

Whether frozen or refrigerated, leave the macarons at room temperature for 1 to 2 hours before serving.

Decor 1
Small sprinkles, nuts and finely chopped tea leaves can be baked on to the shells.

Decor 2
Blow torching shells dusted and baked with sugar adds color and extra crunch.

Decor 3
More adventurous and even savory decorations such as bacon bits may be sprinkled on before baking, resulting in unexpected flavor combinations.

Decor 4
Small stencils that are applied with a spray gun and food coloring can be used to decorate and customize macaron shells.

MACARON MISTAKES

Flat, cracked, sticky, wrinkly, uncooked, tasteless, burned or footless macarons? Simply compare your finished macaron with one of the images below to find out what might be the reason for a macaron gone wrong and how to correct it in your quest for perfection.

••• WHAT WENT WRONG?

CRACKED SHELLS

During baking, air in the meringue component of the batter expands. If an inadequate skin has formed before baking, the batter will expand, rise up and crack the shell. The method described on page 22 will maximize the skin before baking and therefore minimize cracking.

Piping and baking the macarons quickly will also prevent cracking. The texture and integrity of the final batter is at its best while residual heat from the Italian meringue remains.

Shell decorations, particularly nuts, may compromise the skin of the unbaked macaron shell. It may be necessary to add some decorations after baking.

IRREGULARLY SHAPED SHELLS

Perfectly round macron shells are dependent on making a batter that has volume and structure. That structure is achieved by incorporating the correct amount of air. If that is achieved the batter will pipe evenly and naturally settle on the baking sheet into an even round shape. Over-mixing the batter knocks out too much air, causing it to run and seep out into an uneven shape.

Macarons

FLAT OR POORLY RISEN SHELLS

The amount a macaron shell rises during baking is dependent on air incorporated in the batter. This air expands when heated in the oven and causes the shells to rise. Too little air in the mix occurs if the final batter is over-beaten, knocking out the air. It also occurs if the meringue isn't whisked well enough before the ground almond and icing sugar mix is added.

As well as giving rise to poorly risen and irregularly shaped shells, over-mixing the batter can compromise the ability of the unbaked shell to form a skin. This may be another reason why the shells crack during baking.

OVER-RISEN SHELLS OR THOSE WITH AN IRREGULAR SURFACE

This is caused by under-mixing the final batter. It may be corrected before baking by tapping the baking trays on the kitchen surface, encouraging the shells to spread evenly. If you are unsure of your macaron batter consistency and mix, pipe and bake a couple of shells before making and baking them all.

SHELLS STUCK TO THE BAKING TRAY

Piping the macarons onto silicone parchment paper or a silicone mat is the best way of baking them and will help with peeling them off. If they still stick then they may be a little under-baked. Macarons can be returned to the oven for a couple more minutes to help them dry out further, aiding their release.

Running a teaspoon or two of tap water between the baking sheet and paper and leaving it for 5 minutes may help release the shells. The moisture dampens the paper slightly and assists the baked shell with cleaving from the paper. A small offset spatula can also be slid underneath stuck shells to release them.

Macarons

CHOUX PASTRY

Choux pastry's transformation from glossy dough to a voluminous, crunchy pastry shell always amazes and delights. Many cakes and patisserie can be achieved by following meticulous recipes and methods, but a perfect choux also requires judgment and instinct. Making perfect choux pastry is a significant milestone in your patisserie journey.

Good choux pastry is an impressive building block for many cakes. From a simple cream puff to a show-stopping croquembouche, its ability to add texture and flavor is unsurpassed. Choux pastry can be formed and piped into many shapes and sizes, from small balls to elaborate swan shapes, and it should be paired carefully with fillings and frostings.

The contrast between fresh, homemade choux pastry cakes and store-bought éclairs is vast. Choux pastry is at its best for only 4 to 6 hours after it is filled, as it will soften and become damp. If you master the key techniques to make your own choux pastry cakes, you'll never succumb to soggy supermarket éclairs again!

How to Make
BASIC CHOUX PASTRY

Choux pastry is cooked twice. The dough is first cooked on the stove to emulsify the ingredients, then it is shaped and baked in the oven. Crisp, airy shells are dependent on a delicate interplay between air, moisture and protein.

Ingredients

3½ oz (100 g) butter

½ cup (125 ml) milk

½ cup (125 ml) water

2 pinches of salt

½ oz (15 g) superfine sugar

5 oz (150 g) all-purpose flour
   (or 50/50 all-purpose/strong
   white bread-making flour)

approx. 4 medium eggs (see Method),
   plus extra for glazing

Tools

Large mixing bowl

Whisk

Sieve

Method

Step 1

Make sure all your ingredients are at room temperature. Warm the butter in a pot with the milk, water, salt, and sugar. Ensure the liquid doesn't boil until the butter is melted. Once all the butter is melted, bring to the boil for 10 seconds.

Step 2

Remove the pot from the heat and add the flour in one go. Stir slowly to start with to ensure the flour doesn't spill out of the pot, then as the paste comes together, return to a medium heat and cook, stirring all the time. The paste needs to come together as one ball, but it also needs to develop a slight shine or gloss to its surface. This takes 30 to 60 seconds of beating on the heat.

Step 3

Tip the paste into a clean bowl or the bowl of a free-standing mixer and beat for 30 seconds. This cools the paste a little and releases steam. Continue to beat the paste and add the eggs a little at a time. Ensure the paste is smooth and well combined before adding the next amount of egg.

The exact amount of egg required will vary. The final pastry needs to be smooth, glossy and easily piped, but it also needs to be thick enough to support itself. If too much egg is added the pastry will spread after piping, producing flattened and poorly risen choux.

A good way to judge if you have added enough egg is to lift the pastry from the bowl on a large spoon or spatula. The pastry should adhere well to the spatula but then fall back into the bowl with a clean snap. If too little egg is added the pastry won't adhere to the spatula at all; if too much egg is added the pastry will adhere but then quickly run back into the bowl, dripping off the spatula.

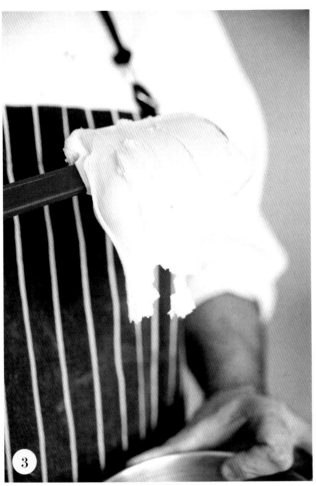

Freezing Choux Pastry

Choux pastry freezes remarkably well. Shaped, unbaked pastry may be frozen for up to a month. Ensure the pastry is completely defrosted before baking. The shells may also be frozen after baking. Defrosting and refreshing them in the oven at 350°F (180°C) for 3 to 4 minutes returns them to their original fresh, crisp form.

Step 4

Preheat the oven to 300°F (150°C) and place an empty metal baking tray in the bottom of the oven.

Piping still warm choux pastry is one of baking's greatest pleasures. Using a piping bag is the best way to shape the pastry for baking, and using a template is a great way of producing uniformly shaped and sized choux buns. Specialist choux pastry silicone trays are also available.

Fit a piping bag with a plain or fluted nozzle approximately 1 inch (2.5 cm) in diameter. Holding the nozzle slightly above the parchment or tray and at a 45° angle, pipe 6-inch (15 cm) lengths of pastry. It helps to stop squeezing the piping bag ½–1 inch (1–2.5 cm) from the end of each éclair and gently flick the end of the nozzle in the opposite direction, cleanly finishing each éclair.

Another technique is to pipe long strips of pastry on a baking sheet and freeze them. Once frozen, the pastry may be cut into precise 6-inch (15 cm) lengths. Allow the pastry to defrost completely before baking.

Once piped, brush the pastry with egg wash to give a glossy finish.

Step 5

Pour two cups of warm water into the baking tray on the bottom of the oven. This creates steam and a humid environment to help the pastry rise. Bake the pastry in the preheated oven for 1 hour. Do not be tempted to open the door to check on them for at least 45 minutes. The drop in temperature and humidity will cause the pastry to collapse.

After 1 hour, check the pastry. The shells should sound hollow when tapped and be an even golden color. If not, return them to the oven and bake for a further 5–10 minutes.

BLACKCURRANT AND LICORICE RELIGIEUSE

This classic French patisserie was popularized by the legendary chef Marie-Antoine Carême. The name refers to the French word for nun.

There's something particularly grown up about the combination of blackcurrant and licorice. The aniseed flavor of the licorice tempers the sweetness of the cake and heightens the fragrance of blackcurrant.

The sablé pastry discs in this recipe produce a choux bun with an even rise, and a crunchy contrast to the soft filling and crisp choux pastry. This basic sablé pastry recipe can be adapted for all choux pastry cakes, including éclairs and cream puffs.

Ingredients

1 quantity of choux pastry, unbaked (see page 38)

Sablé Pastry Discs
3½ oz (100 g) brown sugar
3½ oz (100 g) butter, softened and chopped
4½ oz (125 g) all-purpose flour

Blackcurrant Crème Pâtissière
1 quantity of crème pâtissière (see page 112)
1 cup (250 ml) blackcurrant cordial

Blackcurrant Fondant Frosting
14 oz (400 g) plain fondant frosting (see page 136)
2 tbsp (30 ml) blackcurrant cordial

White Chocolate and Licorice Decoration
3½ oz (100 g) white chocolate, tempered (see page 144)
6–8 of your favorite licorice sweets, chopped into small pieces

Method

1. For the sablé pastry, beat all the ingredients in a mixer until smooth. Wrap the pastry in plastic wrap and refrigerate for 1 to 2 hours.

2. Roll out the pastry to a thickness of about 1/8 inch (2.5 mm). Using a 2½-inch (6 cm) and a 1½-inch (4 cm) pastry cutter, cut out eight discs of each size.

3. For the blackcurrant crème pâtissière, pour the blackcurrant cordial into a small pot and simmer until it has reduced in volume by half. While still warm, mix into the crème pâtissière. Set aside in the refrigerator.

4. For the blackcurrant fondant, warm the fondant in a small pot until it starts to flow. Mix in the cordial. Set aside at room temperature.

5. For the white chocolate decoration, line a baking sheet with parchment paper or preferably an acetate sheet. Mix the finely chopped licorice into the chocolate and spread as a fine layer over the lined baking sheet. As the chocolate cools, cut it into 2-inch (5 cm) squares. Allow to cool completely and set.

6. Line two baking sheets with parchment paper. Using the same pastry cutters as for the sablé discs, draw eight large circles on one baking sheet and eight smaller circles on the second sheet. Preheat the oven to 300°F (150°C).

7. Use a pastry bag with a ½-inch (1 cm) plain round nozzle and fill with the choux pastry. Hold the nozzle approximately 1 inch (2.5 cm) above the center of the circular templates and pipe. The pastry will spread to fill the circle. Once all the large and small templates are filled, place a sablé disc on top of each mound.

8. Bake in the oven for 1 hour. Check they are completely dry and well risen, as described.

9. To assemble the cake, make a small hole in the base of each choux bun using a ½-inch (1 cm) round nozzle. Fill a piping bag with the crème pâtissière and pipe a generous amount into the small and large buns.

10. Warm the blackcurrant fondant frosting again until it flows but still holds it shape in the pot. Invert the filled choux buns into the frosting to coat the tops of the buns. Allow excess frosting to drip back into the pot before turning the right way up and allowing to cool.

11. Place a white chocolate and licorice square on top of the large bun and place the smaller choux bun on top of the square to form the religieuse shape. Finely chop and crumble some of the remaining licorice and chocolate squares and sprinkle over the top of the smaller bun to finish the cake. Store in the refrigerator but serve at room temperature.

THE PERFECT CHOCOLATE ÉCLAIR

Alongside the tarte au citron and the madeleine, the chocolate éclair is a patisserie classic. While relatively straightforward to make, its success depends on the details and perfect execution. The basics of this recipe are easily adapted to incorporate a range of different flavors, textures and decoration.

Ingredients

1 quantity of choux pastry, unbaked (see page 38). Add a little less egg to give a slightly firmer and drier mix to assist with even piping.

Chocolate Crème Pâtissière

$^{2}/_{5}$ cup (100 ml) heavy cream

3½ oz (100 g) dark chocolate (approx. 60 percent cocoa solids), finely chopped

1 quantity of store-bought pâtissière fondant

Chocolate Frosting

10½ oz (300 g) fondant frosting (see page 136)

2 tbsp (30 g) cocoa powder

3–4 tbsp (45–60 ml) water

Method

1. Pipe 12 éclairs following the method on page 39. Brush with beaten egg and bake in an oven set at 300°F (150°C) for 1 hour.

2. Warm the cream in a small pot until it just begins to boil. Pour over the chopped chocolate and stir until smooth. If any lumps of chocolate remain, stick blend the mix until smooth. Combine this chocolate ganache with the crème pâtissière and set aside in the refrigerator until ready to use.

3. Warm the fondant in a small pot until it flows. Stir in the cocoa powder. Add the water a tablespoon at a time until you have a smooth paste.

4. To assemble the éclairs, make three small holes in the base of each éclair with a ½-inch (1 cm) round piping nozzle. Fill a piping bag with the chocolate crème pâtissière and fill the éclairs, starting at one end and moving along to fill the middle and opposite end holes in turn.

5. Ensure the chocolate frosting is still warm and flows. Invert the éclair and dip it into the frosting. Turn the éclair the right way up but held at a 45° angle over the bowl of frosting. Gently run your finger along the top, pushing off any excess. Clean your finger on a cloth then run it along both sides of the frosting to give a clean, even line along the side of the éclair. Refrigerate until ready to serve.

APPLE CRUMBLE AND CUSTARD CARAMEL ÉCLAIRS

Apple crumble and custard paired with salted caramel and encased within the crisp shell of an éclair — what's not to like?

Ingredients

1 quantity of choux pastry, unbaked (see page 38). Add a little less egg to give a slightly firmer and drier mix to assist with even piping.

Crumble Topping
2 oz (50 g) butter
2 oz (50 g) soft brown sugar
2 oz (50 g) all-purpose flour
2 oz (50 g) ground almonds

Salted Caramel Crème Patissière / Caramel Glaze
1 quantity of crème pâtissière (see page 112)
10½ oz (300 g) superfine sugar
1⅕ cups (300 ml) heavy cream
5 oz (150 g) butter
salt, to taste

Apple Compôte
3 large apples (a sharp, firm apple such as a Granny Smith works best for this)
2–3 tbsp (30–45 g) superfine sugar
squeeze of lemon juice

Method

1. Pipe 12 éclairs following the method on page 38. Brush with beaten egg and bake in an oven set at 300°F (150°C) for 1 hour.

2. Preheat the oven to 350°F (180°C). For the crumble topping, place all the ingredients in a food processor and mix with the blade attachment until well combined and small lumps start to form. Alternatively, rub the butter into the flour using your fingertips. Stir in the almonds and sugar and work with a spoon until the small lumps form.

3. Tip out onto a lined baking tray and bake in the oven for 6 to 8 minutes or until golden. Allow the crumble mix to cool. Break up any larger lumps with your fingers.

4. As with every time you make caramel, ensure all your ingredients and equipment are prepared before starting to melt the sugar. Caramelize the sugar in a small pot (see page 146). When the sugar reaches a rich auburn/red color, add the cream and butter. The sugar will solidify, but continue to stir on a medium heat and the sugar will re-melt producing a smooth caramel. Allow the caramel to cook for 30 seconds, then pour into a clean bowl and allow to cool to room temperature.

5. Set aside half of the caramel to glaze the éclairs. Mix the other half of the caramel into the crème pâtissière. Add salt to taste.

6. For the apple compôte, peel, core and chop the apples into ¼-inch (5 mm) cubes. Place these in a pot with a teaspoon of water and a tablespoon of the sugar. Warm gently until the apples begin to soften and break down a little. You are looking for a consistency that can be piped but still retains some texture and bite. You may require an additional teeaspoon or 2 of water to create this texture. Depending on the apples used, you may need to purée some of the apple compote in a food processor to create a mix that is easy to pipe. Check the sweetness of the compôte. It may require a little more sugar or a squeeze of lemon juice. You need something relatively sour to balance the sweeter glaze and crème pâtissière.

7. To assemble the éclairs, make three small holes in the base of each éclair with a ½-inch (1 cm) round piping nozzle. Fill a piping bag with the apple compôte and pipe a small amount into each of the holes.

8. Fill another piping bag with the salted caramel crème pâtissière and fill the éclairs, starting at one end and moving along to fill the middle and opposite end holes in turn.

9. Ensure the caramel glaze is still warm and flows. Invert the éclair and dip it into the glaze. Turn the éclair the right way up but held at a 45° angle over the bowl of glaze. Gently run your finger along the top, pushing off any excess. Clean your finger on a cloth then run it along both sides of the glaze to give an even line along the side of the éclair. Sprinkle with the crumble topping and serve.

CHOUX PASTRY MISTAKES

Choux pastry depends on incorporating just the right amounts of air, moisture and protein into its makeup. If your pastry looks like one of the images below you will be able to identify what went wrong in the process and how you can avoid it the next time round.

• • • WHAT WENT WRONG?

ROOM TEMPERATURE

Make sure all your ingredients are at room temperature. Melting cold butter into the water and milk will take significantly longer, thereby increasing the moisture loss from the mix while the butter melts. This will affect how well the choux pastry rises.

CRACKING

Choux pastry is prone to cracking during baking. Using a higher protein content flour or a 50/50 mix of all-purpose and strong white bread-making flour helps with this as it develops a structure that rises more evenly.

Another helpful technique is to pipe éclairs using a fluted nozzle, which gives a greater surface area to the unbaked éclair, allowing more room for the pastry beneath to rise evenly without cracking. The Ateco range of fluted nozzles work well for this: try numbers 867 or 868.

Choux Pastry

50

POOR RISE

This is the most common problem with choux pastry. Adding too much egg and producing a pastry that is too runny and loose is the most likely cause. Add the egg carefully and slowly. Ensuring the oven is humid during the early stages of baking will also help the pastry rise. The water in the oven delays the crust on the choux bun forming, thereby allowing the pastry to rise further before setting.

UNEVEN SHAPE

The shape of the unbaked choux is magnified during baking. That is, the smallest imperfections in the piping or shaping of the unbaked pastry are exaggerated. Piping choux pastry, as with all piping, is about confidence, preparation and speed. A confident, quick and smooth piping action is much more likely to produce exact and identical results. Freezing and then shaping the pastry is another excellent method of baking evenly shaped éclairs.

Baking the choux pastry with a disc or strip of sablé pastry on top will also help even out the rise (see Blackcurrant and Licorice Religieuse, page 40).

NOT CRISP

The crispness of choux pastry comes from driving the water out of the mix, which only happens if they are baked for long enough in the oven. Every oven is different and some are more efficient than others at releasing humidity and water. If your choux pastry isn't crisping well, you can make small holes in the shells after the first hour of baking and return the shells to the oven. These holes will allow additional moisture to escape and will also serve as the hole through which they can be filled.

... TARTS

This chapter uses a good, all-round sweet shortcrust pastry, pâte sucrée. Other pastries can be used to make sweet tarts, and the recipes will work as well with sablée and brisée. The difference between pastries is in the proportions of sugar and fat in the form of butter. Sablée pastry is a particularly delicate and sweet dough that's almost like a shortbread biscuit. Pâte brisée is more versatile, easier to handle and less sweet.

A round, fluted pastry case is perhaps the most familiar to home bakers. However, sweet pastry should not be confined by predictable tart cases and rings. Straight-sided circular rings instantly give a professional patisserie appearance, while oval- and square-shaped rings and cases are now readily available, as are specialist silicone mats and molds (see Resources, page 156).

Hands vs Machines

For traditionalists, the prospect of using a machine (a mixer or food processor) to make pastry is the stuff of nightmare. But there is a good case for making pastry (and perhaps the majority of the recipes in this book) by hand the first time. Doing so will help you understand the consistencies required. There is no better tool than hands for judging the texture and feel of a mix. Pastry is very easy to over-work, but with time and confidence mixers and food processors will prove valuable time-savers.

How to Make
PÂTE SUCRÉE

This is the basic sweet pastry which forms a delightful base for so many tarts. Once you have mastered the making of it, you will become better aware of the consistency and texture of good pastry, which makes it an excellent place to start.

Ingredients
3½ oz (100 g) butter

2½ oz (65 g) confectioners' sugar

1 vanilla pod

¾ oz (20 g) ground almonds

1½ oz (40 g) whole egg

6 oz (175 g) all-purpose flour

Tools
Large mixing bowl

Food mixer

Bowl scraper

Spatula

Plastic wrap

Rolling pin

Tart ring(s)

Scissors

Fork

Baking beans

Paring knife or
    Microplane grater

Method

Step 1
Make sure all the ingredients are at room temperature. Place the butter and confectioners' sugar in a bowl and mix until well combined, pale and beginning to become fluffy. If using a free-standing mixer, scrape down the sides of the bowl and mix again.

Step 2
Split the vanilla pod and scrape out the seeds, then add the seeds to the butter and sugar. Scrape the sides of the bowl down again and add the ground almonds.

Step 3
Beat the egg and add to the mixture bit by bit, waiting until the previous amount is incorporated before adding the next. It's crucial at this stage to ensure you keep scraping down the sides of the bowl to keep all the ingredients well combined.

Step 4
Add the flour in one go. This step makes the biggest difference to the success or otherwise of the pastry. You need to combine the flour well but quickly. The longer you take to incorporate the flour the greater the chance of developing too much gluten, which will make the

pastry tough. It's easy to over-work the pastry and if you are worried about doing so with a mixer, revert to mixing in the flour by hand with a spatula.

Step 5
Lightly flour the work surface by taking pinches of flour and flicking it across the table. More flour incorporated at this stage and rolling out will toughen the pastry. At this point the pastry may seem too soft and loose (5a), but chilling it will firm it up. Work the pastry with your hand until it comes together as one piece (5b). Shape into a thick round (5c), wrap in plastic wrap and refrigerate for at least 1 hour.

PÂTE SUCRÉE (CONTINUED)

Step 6

Roll the pastry out to a depth of $^1/_8$ inch (3 mm). A light, delicate touch is required here (6a). You need to avoid rolling and re-rolling the pastry, so getting it right the first time makes a difference. Always start with your rolling pin in the center of the pastry and roll to the edge. Don't roll across the entire piece of pastry from one edge to the other as that will create an uneven depth. The longer you take to roll out the pastry, the warmer it will become and more likely to stick to the work surface. If that's a problem the pastry can be rolled out between two large sheets of plastic wrap (6b) until it reaches the desired thickness (6c).

For perfectly even pastry, the final stages of rolling may be done between two $^1/_8$ inch (3 mm) depth strips of stainless steel. Either end of the rolling pin is placed on the metal and the pastry will spread to the correct depth.

Step 7

Well-chilled and evenly rolled pastry can be used in a variety of shapes and sizes. It's personal preference, but tart rings with straight sides produce finished tarts with a professional, clean look. Bottomless tart rings are also easier to use and line than tart cases. Brush your chosen tart ring lightly with melted butter or oil. Dust the ring with flour then tap on the surface to remove any excess. Place on a similarly greased and floured flat baking tray.

Place the tart ring or case on the pastry to judge how much you need: 1–1½ inches (2.5–4 cm) wider than the diameter of the ring is usually enough. For your favorite and regularly used

rings a card template can be drawn so you accurately trim the pastry every time. You need to avoid too much excess pastry as when the pastry is placed over the ring and eased into shape, the excess over the sides will pull and stretch the pastry in the ring.

Step 8

Roll the pastry up around a floured rolling pin and gently rest over the ring. Working quickly, lift the edges of the pastry and gently ease it into the bottom of the ring. If you obviously have too much pastry, roughly trim it with a pair of kitchen scissors. A little pastry hanging over the sides of the ring is ideal, with a final trim once the ring has been baked.

Using a small piece of spare pastry, go around the base of the ring gently pushing the pastry into the right angle between the sides of the ring and tray. Lightly prick the pastry with a fork all over to prevent it rising in the oven. At this stage, resting the pastry again in the refrigerator for 30 minutes will minimize any shrinkage during baking.

Step 9

Preheat the oven to 350°F (180°C). Remove the pastry from the refrigerator and line the pastry case with plastic wrap and baking beans. It is best to layer 3 or 4 pieces of plastic wrap on top of each other for extra strength when lifting the baking beans out after baking. Plastic wrap will shrink and contract but not melt in the heat of the oven. The wrap in contact with the pastry will remain loose. Plastic wrap works better than parchment paper or foil as it's much easier to push it into

the corners of the tart ring, giving an even finish.

Step 10

Bake in the center of the oven for 12 to 18 minutes depending on the size and shape of the ring or case. The base of the pastry case should be an even light brown color. It's tricky to judge when chocolate pastry is correctly baked as it's already brown in color. If you're not sure, take it out of the oven after approximately 15 minutes depending on the size of the case and remove the plastic wrap and baking beans. It can always be returned to the oven again for a few minutes to finish.

Step 11

Remove from the oven and gently lift the plastic wrap and baking beans out. The pastry can be trimmed at this point with either a small sharp paring knife, or for a perfect finish a fine-grade Microplane grater does a brilliant job of trimming evenly.

Tarts

56

TARTE AU CITRON

Alongside the madeleine, the tarte au citron is perhaps the best measure of how good a pastry cook you are. Made well, there is no finer dessert.

You should start out with the perfect baked and trimmed pastry case, but bear in mind that the preparation of the filling requires just as much care and attention. This recipe works best if the filling is part-cooked on the stove before baking, as this reduces the additional pastry baking time and prevents it from being over-cooked. It also helps the lemon filling set evenly. Ideally, this recipe requires an instant-read thermometer to check temperatures. It can be done without temperature checking, but it's easy to over-bake the tart, which spoils the effect and the careful work you've put into making this classic delicacy.

This recipe gives a sharp, zingy finish due to the fresh lemons. If you'd prefer something sweeter, reduce the amount of lemon juice or do not bother infusing the lemon zest into the juice.

Ingredients

1 x 10-inch (25 cm) pâte sucrée
tart case, baked
(see page 54)

zest and juice of 6 lemons
8 eggs
12 oz (340 g) superfine sugar,
plus extra for caramelizing
1 1/8 cups (280 ml) heavy cream

Method

1. Prepare the pâte sucrée case as described on page 54. This case will be baked again with the filling, so it is preferable to slightly under-bake the first time until only the beginnings of the light brown color develop on the base. Brush the tart case with egg wash and return to the oven for 3 to 4 minutes. Place on a lined baking sheet in its case or ring.

2. Preheat the oven to 250°F (120°C). Place the lemon zest and juice in a small pot. Heat and simmer gently until the volume of the juice has reduced by half. Set aside and allow to cool.

3. Beat the eggs and add the sugar. During the preparation of the filling you need to avoid incorporating too much air. Instinctively the whisk may be the tool you reach for to combine; if so, use it gently. Any bubbles in the mix will create a froth, which when poured into the tart compromises its final appearance. Add the cream to the mix.

4. Pour the reduced lemon juice through a small sieve into the cream, eggs and sugar. At this point the mix may appear to briefly curdle. Continue to stir or whisk and the mix will come back together into a thin custard.

5. Pour the custard into a bowl set over a simmering pot of water (bain-marie). Stir and gently warm the mix until it reaches 140°F (60°C), then pour into a jug.

6. Half fill the tart ring with the warm lemon filling and place in the oven on the baking sheet. Carefully pour in the rest of the filling to the top of the case. The filling won't rise so it can be filled as high up the case as you dare. If small bubbles are present and a froth forms on top, they can be removed by a quick blast from a blow torch.

The eggs in the filling will begin to set at 158°F (70°C). The heat in the oven will bring the temperature up, setting the custard from the outside of the case to the center. This will take approximately 15 minutes but check regularly with an instant-read digital thermometer. If judging by appearance, it's ready when the outside of the tart appears set and wobbly but the center is still a little liquid. The residual heat in the mix will continue to cook the filling once it's out of the oven, so don't worry about removing it before it looks completely set.

7. Allow the tart to cool completely. Cut into slices and dust lightly with superfine sugar. Blow torch the slices to create a caramelized effect. The finished tart should be silky smooth, creamy and rich. The filling shouldn't be cracked or come away from the sides of the pastry case. If it is, then it's slightly over-cooked. It will still taste lovely, but be spurred on to try again. You'll know when it's perfect because it will taste remarkable.

Variation

It's easy to change this recipe to include chocolate pastry. Simply replace ¹/₃ oz (10 g) of the all-purpose flour with ¹/₃ oz (10 g) cocoa powder.

PASSION FRUIT, MILK CHOCOLATE AND SALTED CARAMEL TART

This is a grown-up dessert. Any three of the key components work well alone, but as a trio they are a powerhouse of pastry pleasure. The weirdly addictive property of salted caramel is heightened by the milk chocolate and then balanced by the sharp passion fruit. You long for it, are satisfied by it and then refreshed. These work particularly well as small individual tarts.

Ingredients

1 x 10-inch (25 cm) chocolate pâte sucrée tart case or 12 x 3-inch (7 cm) cases, baked (see page 54)

7 oz (200 g) butter, softened

9 oz (250 g) soft light brown sugar

1 cup (250 ml) heavy cream

½ tsp (2.5 g) sea salt

9 oz (250 g) milk chocolate, chopped

½ cup (125 ml) passion fruit purée or juice of 5–6 whole passion fruits, seeds removed

½ tsp (2.5 g) agar-agar

Method

1. Prepare the chocolate pâte sucrée case as described.

2. Place the butter and sugar in a small pot and warm gently until melted. Simmer for 2 minutes. Add the cream and salt and heat to 226°F (108°C) (approximately 5 minutes of gentle warming).

3. Pour the caramel mix over the chocolate and stir until smooth. You need to work quickly to incorporate this mix together and pour into the tart case as it sets quickly. Fill the tart case to the top of the pastry shell.

4. Mix the agar-agar with the cold purée and water in a small pot until the agar agar has dissolved and the mixutre comes to the boil. Immediately pour the purée into the bottom of a small dish or bowl so it forms a depth of ¼–½ inch (5–10 mm). Place in the refrigerator to set. When firm, chop into small ¼-inch (5 mm) cubes and sprinkle over the top of the tart.

STRAWBERRY, PINK PEPPERCORN AND WHITE CHOCOLATE TART

The spiced fragrance of the pink peppercorn works beautifully with fresh strawberries, while the accompanying white chocolate filling soothes and complements the fruit. The color contrast between the pale white chocolate and the pink strawberries is reason alone to make this.

Ingredients

1 x 10-inch (25 cm) pâté sucrée tart case or 12 x 3-inch (7 cm) cases, baked (see page 54)

10½ oz (300 g) strawberries

2 tbsp (30 g) crushed pink peppercorns or 3 pinches of ground black pepper

1 tsp (5 g) pectin

2 tbsp (30 g) superfine sugar

squeeze of lemon juice

or

½ jar of your favorite strawberry jelly seasoned with black pepper to taste.

1½ cup (350 ml) heavy cream

13 oz (360 g) white chocolate, chopped

3½ oz (100 g) butter, softened

a few fresh strawberries/ crushed pink peppercorns, chopped pistachios to decorate

Method

1. Prepare the pâté sucrée tart case as described.

2. Wash and hull the strawberries, removing the leaves and pale top underneath, then purée them in a food processor or by chopping finely and then sieving. Place the purée in a small pot and add the peppercorns. Gently warm the purée until it just simmers, then set aside and allow the pepper flavor to infuse for 30 minutes.

3. Sieve out the peppercorns. Mix the powdered pectin with the sugar and then stir into the purée. Heat the mix until it bubbles and cook for 30 seconds. This is important to allow the pectin to thicken the purée. Let the purée cool then spoon into the base of the tart case. Place the tart in the refrigerator to allow the purée to firm up before pouring the chocolate layer on top.

4. Warm the cream in a pot until almost boiling then pour over the chocolate. Leave the hot cream to melt the chocolate for a minute and then stir until smooth. If any lumps of chocolate remain it can be stick blended briefly. When cool, mix in the butter. Pour the chocolate mix over the strawberry layer and allow to set at room temperature.

5. Decorate with more slices of strawberries, pink peppercorns (to taste), and pistachios, and serve at room temperature.

TART MISTAKES

Getting pastry just right can be tricky, especially in the beginning. If your tart crust has not come out the way you expected it to, see if any of the problems and their solutions on these pages provide an answer. With a few tweaks to your method, the problem is solved.

••• WHAT WENT WRONG?

ROOM TEMPERATURE

Making sure all the ingredients are at room temperature really does make a difference here. In particular, combining cold eggs and butter in this recipe is difficult.

If you choose to ignore this, either through impatience or for the love of a challenge, then there are tricks that can assist. Chopping the butter into small cubes and beating (preferably with a free-standing mixer) for a few minutes will help warm up the butter. Similarly, warming the bowl slightly by rinsing it with boiling water then drying will help soften it. Microwaving butter is a dark art, but if you must, do so in 5-second bursts and keep a close eye on it.

SHRINKAGE

Pastry may shrink during baking. This occurs when the gluten in the pastry contracts. Trimming the pastry case after baking can help with this. Being mindful of not over-working the pastry and developing too much gluten will also help.

Resting and relaxing the pastry in the refrigerator or even freezer will also help. This is vital after the initial mixing of the pastry, but can also help after the pastry has been rolled and used to line the ring or case. Baking the pastry direct from the refrigerator or freezer will take longer but works well.

HOLES

Try to cut the correct amount of pastry to line the ring or case and keep the pastry chilled. Rolling out the pastry evenly and quickly helps. Holes occur when the pastry is stretched or roughly handled. Small holes before baking can be fixed with spare pastry. With larger holes it's often best to re-chill the pastry and then try again. Holes after baking can be filled with raw pastry if the filling of the case is to be baked.

With liquid tart fillings that require baking, it's best to assume a small hole might be there and egg wash the case. Brush a lightly beaten egg around the base and sides of the case and then bake 3 to 4 minutes at 350°F (180°C). This will seal the case. It might seem unnecessary, but scraping leaked tart filling from the bottom of your oven is no fun.

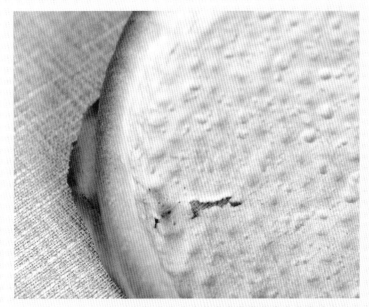

UNDER-BAKING

The most common pastry mistake is to under-bake it. The pastry is ready when the base of the case is a light golden brown in color. Don't judge whether the pastry is cooked by looking at the edges of the case as they brown earlier than the base.

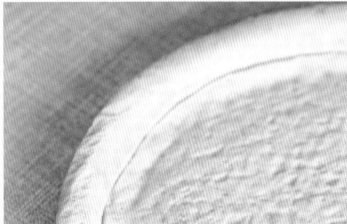

OVER-BAKING

After approximately 10 minutes of baking, the pastry structure and shape will be set. It is therefore possible to remove the plastic wrap and baking beans and keep a closer eye on the pastry as it turns golden-brown in the heat. This will help prevent over-baking.

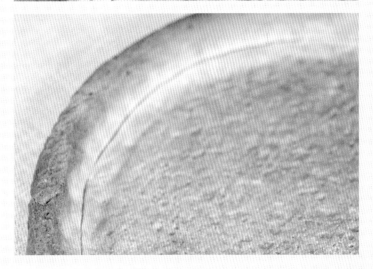

... GÂTEAUX & ENTREMETS

This is where you can start to have some real fun. These cakes allow you to combine the fillings and finishes you've learned in this book into grand adventures of flavor, texture and flamboyant decoration. Remember: the golden rule of gâteaux is that they must be just a little bit over the top.

Gâteaux and entremets are terms often used interchangeably to refer to an extravaganza of a cake with layers of sponge, creams, ganaches and fruit that is highly decorated and precisely finished. These cakes are usually made as one and then cut into individual portions. Gâteaux are generally thought of as layers of sponge, flavored creams and fruit. Historically, entremets have simply meant a dessert course, but more recently have been used to describe layered cakes with varying textures.

Although the flavor of the gâteau is important, texture is perhaps more so. These cakes are often cut as tall slices, and without textural contrast they would become monotonous and tiresome. Each component should come alive as you eat it. It's the hidden details of these cakes that makes them special. Secreting little pockets of contrasting flavored mousse, a sharp-tasting fruit gel or perhaps explosive popping candy adds drama and excitement.

BUILDING YOUR OWN GÂTEAUX

Here's where all your latent building ambitions can be realized in cake form. The design, planning and architecture of these cakes make the difference between subsidence-prone wonky structures and glorious, upright skyscrapers. Firm foundations, even layers and careful construction are key.

FIRM FOUNDATIONS AND EVEN LAYERS

The base of the gâteau is the last component your knife will slice through when portioned. It therefore needs to cut cleanly and sharply. A well-made sponge or a component that uses chocolate to bind works best. Similarly, perfectly baked sweet or puff pastry can achieve the same effect. As with all the layers the base needs to be carefully leveled and even. A gentle touch with the rolling pin or meticulous work with an offset spatula are key skills.

CLEAN EDGES

These cakes are showy and will demonstrate how good a pastry cook you are. The world needs to see the care you've taken over layering and finishing the cake. Building the cake within a boundary lined by acetate is a wonderful way of finishing a cake. Once finished and chilled, the acetate strip can be peeled away to reveal a perfectly smooth, clean and even edge.

After construction these cakes need to be left alone to settle and cool. They are almost always better portioned and cut after they have been chilled overnight in a refrigerator. Some benefit from being frozen, portioned and allowed to defrost before serving.

USING FRAMES AND MOLDS

There is a huge range of silicone and metal frames and molds for cake construction, both for larger cakes and individual versions (see Resources, page 156). Traditional metal cake tins also work well. The best starting point is a simple shape, whether oblong, square or circle.

When ambition kicks in, try to stick to molds and frames that allow your cake rather than the clever mold to be the star. Keep it simple.

CUTTING CAKES

As with all knife work, use the knife you are friendliest with and feel most comfortable using. Cutting clean, straight lines takes a bit of practice and the right tools but it gives a professional-looking finish.

TIPS FOR SUCCESS

Choose a knife that is long enough to cut through the entire gâteau in one hand action.

Place the cake on an even flat surface that allows you to push the knife all the way to the base. Give yourself room. An errant elbow that hits a refrigerator door or a hungry guest peering over your shoulder will ruin your smooth slicing.

Repeated slicing or sawing actions will unsettle your carefully prepared layers. Use one smooth movement. Often the base is thicker and more substantial, so check the edge of the blade is flush with the chopping board at the front and back of the cut cake. Once through to the base don't pull the knife straight out as this will drag and merge the layers of the cake. Pull the knife to one side, separating the cake into two pieces on the board. Remarkably this technique alone can make the difference between an exceptional and average-looking cake.

The Right Equipment

Having the right kind of knife makes a great deal of difference in the finished presentation of your cakes. A long, straight knife that has recently been sharpened will ensure clean cuts and lines and will give the professional touch to your baking.

Gâteaux & Entremets

71

How to Make
GENOISE SPONGE

Baked as thin sheets of sponge, this is easily cut to size and can be stored frozen. Genoise works particularly well if it's allowed to dry almost to the point of stale for a few days, as it can then be soaked with sweet syrups or fruit juices.

Ingredients

9 oz (250 g) (approx.
  5 medium) whole eggs
3½ oz (100 g) superfine sugar
3½ oz (100 g) all-purpose flour
1 oz (25 g) butter, melted

Tools

Bain-marie or metal bowl and pot
Whisk
Free-standing food mixer or electric
  whisk
Large spoon or scraper
Pastry tin

Method

Step 1
Combine the eggs and sugar in a bowl. Place the bowl over a pot of simmering water (bain-marie) and continue to whisk. Heat gently while whisking until the mixture becomes thick and pale and reaches 110°F (45°C).

Step 2
Preheat the oven to 340°F (170°C). Transfer the mix to a free-standing mixer or use an electric hand whisk. Continue to whisk until tripled in volume and cooled.

Step 3
Fold in the flour in 2 to 3 additions. Sieve each addition into the mix to evenly distribute the flour over the surface of the egg mix. It is very easy to clump the flour together and this will prevent that. How well you fold the flour through will determine the success of the sponge. It's a delicate balance of incorporating the flour but not knocking too much air out of the mix. Once the flour is incorporated, fold through the melted butter.

Step 4
Pour the mix into a tin lined with silicone paper or onto a flat lined baking sheet. Bake in the oven for 10 to 12 minutes until evenly browned and springy to touch.

Variation

For chocolate genoise, replace ¾ oz (20 g) of flour with cocoa powder.

How to Make
DACQUOISE

Dacquoise adds crunch, and when layered with creams and mousses it softens over time to a marshmallow-like texture. Dacquoise is usually piped or spread into the final required shaped; however, it may be part-baked, cut to size and then returned to the oven to dry and crisp.

Ingredients

7 oz (200 g) ground almonds

2 tbsp (30 g) corn starch

7 oz (200 g) egg whites

7 oz (200 g) superfine sugar

Tools

Baking sheet

Silicone paper

Large spoon or bowl scraper

Whisk

Piping bag and plain round nozzle

Method

Step 1

Preheat the oven to 210°F (100°C). Line a baking sheet with silicone paper. If necessary, draw an outline of the shape you require.

Step 2

Mix the ground almonds and corn starch together. Whisk the egg whites briefly then add the superfine sugar and whisk to stiff peaks. Fold in the ground almonds and corn starch.

Step 3

Pipe the mix, using a plain round nozzle, into the shape required. It may also be spread thinly on a lined baking sheet before part-baking and cutting into the shape required. Bake for 1½ to 2 hours until evenly browned and crisp.

Gâteaux & Entremets

How to Make
JOCONDE

Joconde has more intrinsic flavor than the plainer genoise. It uses ground almonds, which helps it to remain moist and soft. It's particularly flexible and can be used to wrap around gâteaux. It is the key component in the classic Opéra cake.

Ingredients

3½ oz (100 g) superfine sugar

1½ oz (40 g) (2 medium) egg yolks

1½ oz (40 g) ground almonds

2 oz (50 g) all-purpose flour

2½ oz (70 g) (2 medium) egg white

Tools

Baking sheet

Silicone paper

Free-standing mixer

Large mixing bowl

Whisk

Cookie cutters

Method

Step 1

Preheat the oven to 340°F (170°C). Line the baking sheet with silicone paper.

Step 2

Combine half the superfine sugar and the egg yolks in the bowl of a free-standing mixer. Whisk until pale and fluffy. Add the ground almonds and flour and fold through until well combined.

Step 3

In a clean bowl whisk the egg whites for 30 seconds and then add the remaining superfine sugar. Whisk until you have soft peaks. Fold one-third of the meringue into the almond and flour mix to loosen it a little. Gently fold the remaining meringue in and then spread onto the lined baking tray.

Step 4

Bake for 10–12 minutes until evenly browned and springy to the touch. When cooled, cut to the shape required.

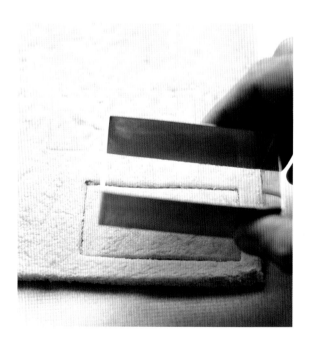

How to Make

DARK CHOCOLATE MOUSSE

Freshly made with the minimum of ingredients, mousses add depth and rich flavor to gâteaux and other cakes. On the following pages are three variants that can be made quickly, with the dark chocolate and fruit mousse being ready to eat immediately.

Ingredients

2 cups (500 ml) heavy cream

7 oz (200 g) dark chocolate

2½ oz (75 g) (approx. 4) egg yolks

2¼ oz (65 g) superfine sugar

⅕ cup (50 ml) water

Tools

Large mixing bowl

Whisk or free-standing mixer

Bain-marie or metal bowl and pot

Small pot

Confectioner's thermometer

Bowl scraper

Method

Step 1
Whisk the cream to soft peaks. It's important to go no further than that or it will make incorporating the chocolate impossible.

Step 2
Melt the chocolate in a bowl over a pot of water (bain-marie) and then allow it to cool. The chocolate needs to be 113°F (45°C) when added to the cream. Keep the pot of water used to melt the chocolate to hand so you can quickly pop the chocolate back on the pot to hold the temperature.

Step 3
Place the egg yolks in the bowl of a free-standing mixer or use a bowl and hand whisk. Whisk the yolks for 10 seconds and set aside.

Step 4
To make the pâte à bombe, warm the sugar and water in a small pot. The mix needs to create a good depth in the pot otherwise it will cook too quickly and make measuring its temperature tricky. If you don't have a small enough pot, it's easier to make twice the quantity of pâte à bombe and only use half. Heat the

sugar syrup to 248°F (120°C). As it gets close to that mark, start to whisk the egg yolks again. As the sugar hits 248°F (120°C), pour it onto the egg yolks and continue to whisk until thickened, cool and airy. This will take 4 to 5 minutes in a free-standing mixer.

Step 5
Now stand tall and take a deep breath. You need to combine the chocolate at 113°F (45°C) with the softly whipped cream. Hold a whisk in your dominant hand and hold the bowl with the melted chocolate in your other hand. Pour

the melted chocolate onto the cream, whisking confidently as you go. For the first 3 to 4 seconds it will look like a disaster, but keep whisking. Scrape the sides of the bowl because the chocolate will cool quickly there and set. You should end up with pale chocolate-colored cream. Then fold through the pâte à bombe and the mousse is ready to use or to be eaten straight from the bowl with a big spoon.

Top Tip

The tricky part in making a mousse is combining the melted chocolate and whipped cream. The temperature of the chocolate when added to the cream needs to be exact. If the chocolate is too hot it will melt the cream; if too cold it will set and become grainy. Concentrate on that stage and the rest is straightforward.

How to Make

WHITE CHOCOLATE MOUSSE

A subtle mousse that takes a little longer to set but cuts cleanly in a gâteau or entremet. It adds a gentle ivory shade to a cake and is particularly good paired with flavors such as lemon, bay and cardamom, which can be infused into the milk before using.

Ingredients
1⅛ cups (280 ml) heavy cream
8 oz (225 g) white chocolate
⅖ cup (100 ml) milk
3½ oz (100 g) (approx. 3) egg white

Tools
Free-standing mixer or hand mixer
Bain-marie or metal bowl and pot
Whisk
Bowl scraper

Method

Step 1
Whip the cream to soft peaks and set aside.

Step 2
Melt the chocolate in a bowl set on a pot of simmering water (bain-marie). Warm the milk and pour onto the melted chocolate to thin it slightly.

Step 3
Whisk the egg whites to soft peaks but no more. If they become stiff and grainy they won't mix with the chocolate easily.

In stages, gently fold the egg whites into the chocolate. Once almost incorporated, start to fold in the softly whipped cream. Leave to set for at least 4 hours, or preferably overnight in a refrigerator.

Gâteaux & Entremets

78

How to Make
FRUIT MOUSSE

This mousse doesn't use chocolate so it needs a little gelatin to help it set and support itself in a cake. The quality of the fruit purée used will determine how good your mousse is. Soft summer fruits puréed with a hand-held blender work perfectly here.

Ingredients

0.4 oz (10 g) silver leaf gelatin

10½ oz (300 g) fruit purée

10½ oz (300 g) whipping cream

3½ oz (100 g) (approx. 3) egg white

10½ oz (300 g) superfine sugar

2½ oz (70 g) water

Tools

Small bowl

1 medium and 1 small pot

Whisk

Free-standing mixer

Confectioner's thermometer

Bowl scraper

Method

Step 1

Soak the gelatin in a small bowl of cold water until soft, jelly-like and pliable. Warm (but don't boil) the fruit purée in a pot. Add the gelatin and let it dissolve into the purée. Remove from the heat and allow to cool.

Step 2

Whisk the cream to soft peaks and set aside.

Step 3

Make an Italian meringue. Place the egg whites in the bowl of a free-standing mixer. Heat the superfine

sugar and water in a small pot until the syrup reaches 242°F (117°C). As the syrup comes up to temperature, start whisking the egg whites. Pour the sugar syrup in a thin stream onto the egg whites and continue to whisk until stiff and cool.

Step 4

Pour the purée over the meringue and fold together. Once blended, fold in the cream. This works perfectly as a dessert in itself, but as with the other mousses may be piped and spread into the range of gâteaux and cakes.

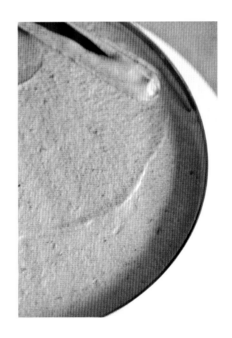

Gâteaux & Entremets

GREEN TEA, WHITE CHOCOLATE AND LEMON DELICE

The success of a fragrant gâteau depends on the freshness of the herbs and lemons. You'll need lemons that make your tongue quiver with excitement. Matcha, a Japanese ceremonial tea with a unique taste and an extraordinary color, adds an alluring and bitter note.

Ingredients

1 sheet of genoise (see page 72), flavored with matcha

1 quantity of lemon curd (see page 128)

1 quantity of white chocolate mousse (see page 78), flavored with bay and cardamom

Extra matcha powder for decoration

Top Tip

These recipes show how components from this book can be combined to create excitement. All the recipes can be made as large cakes or cut and decorated as individual portions.

Method

1. The genoise needs to be flavored with matcha. For beginner genoise bakers it's probably easiest to make plain genoise and soak it with matcha. Make a thin matcha tea using 1 teaspoon (5 g) of matcha, 1 teaspoon (5 g) of superfine sugar and $^{1}/_{3}$ cup (80 ml) of hot water. Bake the genoise as above. Allow to cool and then cut to the size of the tin. Place at the bottom of the tin and soak liberally with the tea.

The matcha powder can also be incorporated directly into the sponge by sifting it together with the flour. For the genoise recipe above add 2 teaspoons (10 g) of matcha.

2. Pour the lemon curd on top of the matcha genoise and place in the refrigerator to cool and set a little. You need a layer approximately ½ inch (1 cm) deep.

3. Make the white chocolate mousse infused with bay and cardamom. Crush 6 cardamom pods and add the seeds and 2 bay leaves to the $^{2}/_{5}$ cup (100 ml) of milk. Bring the milk to a boil and then remove from the heat and allow the flavors to infuse for 30 minutes. Finish the mousse following the recipe above. Pour the mousse on top of the lemon curd layer. Smooth the mousse and return to the refrigerator to set overnight.

4. Cut the delice into perfect oblongs or squares and finish by making a thin paste with some more matcha and water, and brushing over the surface of the cake.

BLACK FOREST BÛCHE CAKE

Take a black forest gâteau and roll it up. The flavors and textures here are simple — chocolate and cherries, mousse and sponge — so they need to be perfect and well balanced to bring the cake alive. The cherry pie filling might sound a bit incongruous and you could make it from fresh cherries, but it would take twice as long and not taste any better.

Ingredients

1 quantity of chocolate genoise (see Variation, page 72)
1 quantity of dark chocolate mousse (see page 76)
1 quantity of chocolate mirror glaze (see page 131)
2 tins of cherry pie filling
Fresh cherries, for decoration

Method

1. Prepare the genoise sponge and chocolate mousse as described.

2. Tip the cherry pie filling into a sieve and allow the cherry juice to drain away. Check a cherry for seasoning. They may require a squeeze of lemon juice or a sprinkle of sugar to bring their flavor back to life. (continued on page 84)

Method

(continued from page 82)

3. Line the curved sides of a specialist 10-inch (25 cm) U-shaped terrine mold with a sheet of acetate cut exactly to size. Spread a little mousse in an even layer approximately ½ inch (1 cm) deep on the sides of the acetate-lined mold.

4. Spread more mousse on the cooled chocolate genoise, again approximately ½ inch (1 cm) deep, then stud the mousse with the tinned cherries. Working from the short side, roll the genoise, mousse and cherries up into a tight cylinder. Mousse will seep out and heart rates will race but all will be well. Trim the rolled mouse and sponge to a size that will fit the lined mold. It doesn't matter if it's a little smaller as it will be covered with more mousse.

5. Gently lower the rolled sponge, mousse and cherries into place and cover with more mousse on top. Run your spatula along the top of the mold to neaten it up and give an even, flat surface. Leave in the freezer overnight.

6. The following day, re-heat your chocolate mirror glaze to 95°F (35°C). De-mold the bûche cake and place it flat-side-down on a wire cooling rack over a tray. Pour the mirror glaze over the cake ensuring an even covering. Decorate with fresh cherries and/or chantilly cream (see page 116).

RASPBERRY AND PISTACHIO GÂTEAU

Raspberries have an unsurpassed ability to complement other sweet flavors. Their fragrant sweet and sour tang works well in a range of cakes. Try raspberry with rose and lychee in the Pierre Hermé classic Ispahan, the pinnacle of flavor combinations.

Ingredients

1 quantity of joconde sponge
  (see page 74), flavored
  with pistachios
1 quantity of white chocolate
  ganache (see page 118),
  flavored with almond
  and pistachios
a few drops of almond
  extract
1 quantity of raspberry
  mousse (see page 79)
2½ oz (75 g) pistachios,
  processed to a fine dust
  in a food processor
7 oz (200 g) whole pistachios
40 (approx.) fresh
  raspberries
confectioners' sugar, to dust

Method

1. Replace the ground almonds in the joconde recipe with 1½ oz (40 g) of the processed pistachios. Bake the joconde and allow to cool.

2. Make the white chocolate ganache, incorporating a few drops of almond extract and the remaining finely ground pistachios. The almond extract heightens the pistachio flavor.

3. Line an 8-inch (20 cm) round cake ring or tin with a removable base with acetate. Cut out a circle of the joconde sponge to fit neatly in the bottom of the tin. Spread the white chocolate ganache on top of the sponge base and allow to set at room temperature.

4. Make the fruit mousse following the recipe on page 79 and using a raspberry purée. The purée can be made from store-bought frozen raspberries, defrosted and puréed in a food processor. Pour the mousse on top of the ganache and spread evenly. Freeze the gâteau overnight.

5. The following day, remove the gâteau from the ring or tin and peel off the acetate. Finely chop the whole pistachio nuts. Carefully press the pistachios around the side of the cake until evenly covered. Decorate the top of the gâteau with as many raspberries as you can and dust with confectioners' sugar.

PETITS FOURS & OTHER SMALL CAKES

Petits fours are the definition of a sweet treat. Elegant two- or three-mouthful cakes, they are usually served at the end of a meal or presented as the focus of a lazy afternoon tea. Petits fours should be delicate and simple rather than grand cakes that demand everyone's attention. Unfussy flavors work best here, and should be combined with light textures and finishes.

Petits fours work well alongside small pieces of confectionery or chocolate. Think of them as small jewels to be gathered and arranged on plates. Identical petits fours may be presented in uniform rows and blocks for added impact.

FINANCIERS (FRIANDS)

Created by a Parisian baker working in the financial heart of Paris, these cakes are named for their appearance, which resembles that of a gold bar.

••• DEFINITION

SHAPE
Although traditionally baked in oblong molds, they can be formed into a variety of shapes. Usually baked in circular or oval molds, friands are the popular Australian and New Zealand version of the same cake.

FLAVOR
Financiers are flavored and enriched with beurre noisette (brown butter), which gives them a smooth finish and a slightly nutty taste. One of the best aspects of financiers is how well they can be adapted. A basic financier mix can be altered to incorporate a range of fragrances and textures, while whole fruits and nuts can be baked into the mix to create pockets of fresh flavor.

BATTER
Financier batter is better when given time to cool and firm up in the refrigerator overnight. It may be baked straight away, but it is runny and a little more difficult to pipe the mix into molds.

Beurre Noisette, Brown Butter

Using beurre noisette in cakes is a way of adding a rich, nutty taste, complementing cakes that use brown sugars or spices such as cloves, cinnamon and nutmeg. It can be made in advance and stored in the refrigerator.

Warm the butter in a pot. It will melt and begin to foam and slowly the milk solids will begin to brown, changing the color of the foam and giving a nutty aroma. When the foam subsides the butter is ready. Remove the pot from the heat and allow to cool. The milk solids sink to the bottom of the hot butter like wine sediment. These solids may be filtered out using a sieve lined with paper towel if desired.

How to Make
BASIC FINANCIERS

Ingredients

2 oz (50 g) all-purpose flour

2 oz (50 g) ground almonds

½ tsp (2.5 g) baking powder

4½ oz (125 g) superfine sugar

⅖ cup (100 ml) liquid beurre
   noisette (see page 90)

3½ oz (100 g) egg white

Tools

Sieve

Large mixing bowl

Wooden spoon or mixing spatula

Piping bag and ½-inch (1 cm)
   plain round nozzle

Financier mold

Method

Step 1

Sift the flour, almonds and baking powder into a bowl and stir in the sugar. Stir in the beurre noisette until a thick paste forms. Add the egg whites gradually to the mix until smooth. Ideally refrigerate the batter overnight.

Step 2

Heat the oven to 350°F (180°C). Fit a piping bag with a ½-inch (1 cm) plain round nozzle and fill with the batter. Fill each financier mold half to two-thirds full.

   If the batter hasn't been chilled it will be runny, and it may help to control the flow if you pinch the piping bag shut just above the nozzle. If not the batter is likely to run over the sides of the mold.

Step 3

Bake for 10 to 12 minutes until well risen, golden brown and springy to the touch. Financiers are best eaten within a few hours of baking while they are light, fresh and if possible still warm.

••• VARIATIONS

RASPBERRIES AND OTHER FRUIT

Push 2 to 3 whole fresh raspberries into the batter-filled molds and bake immediately. If you wish, the fruit may be added halfway through baking as this keeps it raised from the batter.

The same method works for blueberries, apple and pineapple, although very wet and juicy fruits such as strawberries may release too much water during baking and affect the final consistency of the cake.

NUTS

Whole or coarsely chopped nuts can be sprinkled over the surface of the filled mold prior to baking. Hazelnuts, macadamia and pistachio nuts work particularly well. The ground almonds in the basic mix above may be replaced with nut flours. Nut flours can be bought or made by blitzing the same quantity of whole nuts in a food processor with the superfine sugar and flour.

OTHER

Vanilla seeds, citrus fruit zest and a pinch of cinnamon, ginger or cloves can be added to the batter to add fragrance and flavor.

MADELEINES

This scallop-shaped cake epitomizes classic French patisserie. Eaten fresh from the oven, they are unsurpassed. Combine the ingredients using a stiff metal whisk. Quickly and effectively mixing them together helps create a delicate, moist texture.

Ingredients

3 eggs

5 oz (150 g) superfine sugar

⅕ cup (50 ml) milk

6 oz (175 g) all-purpose flour

1½ tsp (7.5 g) baking powder

7 oz (200 g) melted butter

Method

1. Prepare all the ingredients before combining. Use a silicone madeleine tray, or if using a metal tray lightly butter and flour the tray; ensure the scallop-shaped grooves are still prominent and not over-filled with butter and flour. Preheat the oven to 450°F (230°C).

2. Beat the eggs in a large bowl then whisk in the sugar and milk until well combined. Whisk in the flour and baking powder until the batter is smooth, but don't over-work the mix as this will develop the gluten in the flour and toughen the madeleines. Whisk in the butter.

3. Fit a piping bag with a plain nozzle ⅓ inch (8 mm) in diameter and fill with batter. The smaller nozzle will help control the flow of this loose batter as you pipe it into the molds. Half fill each scallop-shaped mold.

4. Bake for 6 to 8 minutes in the very hot oven, preferably turning the tray by 180° halfway through baking.

Variations and Decorations

Finely zested orange or lemon may be added to the mix before baking. A teaspoon (5 g) of matcha green tea adds a complex, bitter note.

After baking, madeleines may be glazed. Warm your favorite honey until liquid and dip the top (not the scalloped side) into the liquid. Return them to the hot oven for 60 seconds to create a crunchy glaze. A lemon or orange glaze can be made by mixing freshly squeezed lemon or orange juice with twice the weight of superfine sugar.

Petits Fours & Other Small Cakes

How to Make
SABLÉS

Uncomplicated and unfussy, these cookies are simple, sweet and buttery. They are best eaten with a cup of tea or alongside a creamy iced dessert.

Ingredients

5½ oz (160 g) butter

2½ oz (75 g) superfine sugar

¾ oz (20 g / 1 medium) egg yolk

1 vanilla pod

7 oz (200 g) all-purpose flour

Variation

for chocolate cookies, replace ⅓ oz (10 g) flour with cocoa powder

Method

Step 1

Start with all the ingredients at room temperature. Mix the butter and sugar together until light and fluffy.

Step 2

Add the egg yolk and vanilla and mix again until smooth. Scrape down the sides of the bowl to ensure everything is mixed well.

Step 3

Add the flour and mix until just combined. Shape into a small ball and cover in plastic wrap. Refrigerate for at least 30 minutes.

Step 4

Preheat the oven to 350°F (180°C). Roll out to a depth of ¼ inch (5 mm) and cut out your chosen shapes. Place on a lined baking sheet and bake in the oven for 10 to 12 minutes until an even light brown color.

SABLÉS VIENNOIS (VIENNESE COOKIES)

These beautifully light, buttery and crumbly cookies are made using similar ingredients to the straightforward sablé, but the superfine sugar is swapped for confectioners' sugar and egg yolk replaced with egg white. The butter must be really soft or the mix will be too stiff to pipe. It's preferable to make the mix too loose and let it firm up a bit before piping than struggling with burst piping bags.

Ingredients

7 oz (200 g) butter, very soft

2½ oz (75 g) confectioners' sugar

1½ oz (40 g) (1 medium) egg white

1 vanilla pod

7 oz (200 g) all-purpose flour

Method

1. Cream the super-soft butter with the confectioners' sugar until light and fluffy. Gradually add the egg white and continue to beat. You may need to whisk the mix briefly to bring it all together.

2. Split the vanilla pod and scrape out the seeds. Add the seeds to the egg, sugar and butter mix. Mix in the flour but only enough to combine — any more and the cookies will become chewy and tough.

3. Preheat the oven to 350°F (180°C) and line a baking sheet. Fit a piping bag with a ½-inch (1 cm) star-shaped nozzle and fill with the cookie mix. Pipe in a zig-zag from left to right covering a space 1½–2 inches (4–5 cm). After piping the biscuits, place the tray in the fridge for 15 minutes. Baking them cold will help the biscuits keep their shape. Bake in the oven for 10 to 12 minutes until an even light brown.

TUILES

These are simple, snappy cookies. Keep them thin and delicately flavored with the zest of a lemon or orange or a few drops of vanilla extract. They are perfect wedged in the top of an ice cream sundae.

Ingredients

2½ oz (70 g) butter

2½ oz (70 g) confectioners' sugar

2½ oz (70 g) (2 medium) egg white

2½ oz (70 g) all-purpose flour

Method

1. Melt the butter in a small pot then combine with the confectioners' sugar in a bowl.

2. Whisk in the egg whites until smooth and then add the flour. At this point add any flavorings. Leave to firm up for 20 minutes in the refrigerator. The mix needs to be loose enough to spread to a thin layer, but also firm enough to hold its shape.

3. Preheat the oven to 350°F (180°C). Spread the mix thinly and evenly into 3 inch (7 cm) diameter circles no more than ½₄ inch (1 mm) deep.

4. Bake in the oven for 6 to 8 minutes. The tuiles are ready when just beginning to brown around the edges. Remove from the oven and lift the tuiles immediately onto a rolling pin to form a curved shape. Allow to cool on the rolling pin until firm and crisp.

Petits Fours & Other Small Cakes

MAKES 18

ARLETTE COOKIES

In this recipe, layers of thinly rolled puff pastry are dredged in sugar and baked. As you bite into the cookie it disintegrates into hundreds of tiny pieces of crispy, caramelized sugar and pastry. Simple and perfecton their own, they are also wonderful paired with creamy desserts such as crème caramels or custards. Two arlettes can be used to sandwich together a filling, perhaps a spoonful of ice cream or sweetened mascarpone and fresh berries.

Ingredients

9 oz (250 g) puff pastry
(store-bought)

7 oz (200 g) confectioners'
sugar, plus extra for rolling
out the pastry

Method

1. Lightly dust the work surface with confectioners' sugar and roll out the block of pastry to a rough rectangle approximately ⅛ inch (2.5 mm) in depth. Trim this shape to a neat rectangle approximately 6 x 12 inches (15 x 30 cm). Very lightly brush the pastry with water. This will help the pastry stick together as it's rolled up.

2. With the long side in front of you, start to slowly roll the pastry into a tube. It may be helpful to pinch the first roll of the pastry together to create a core that the rest of the pastry can roll around. Wrap the roll in plastic wrap and refrigerate until firm.

3. Preheat the oven to 400°F (200°C). Sift the confectioners' sugar into a bowl.

4. Cut the pastry roll into ¼-inch (5 mm) slices. Lay each slice flat in front of you. Using a rolling pin, roll out the slices in one direction to create oval shapes approximately ⅛ inch (2.5 mm) thick. If you want a neater finish the arlette can be cut out at this stage with a small fluted pastry cutter. Drop each rolled-out slice into the confectioners' sugar and ensure it's well covered on both sides. Place the arlette on a lined baking sheet and bake for 5 to 6 minutes or until an even golden color.

MERINGUES

The best way to achieve a stand-alone meringue delicacy is to bake a meringue with a soft and preferably chewy center. A monotonous dry meringue that explodes at first bite is no fun. Instead, think crisp, sugary tectonic plate that collapses into marshmallowy moistness. Modern flavorings, freeze-dried fruits and decorations allow for a wide range of different meringues.

The recipe below is a mix of Italian and French meringue. The sugar is warmed but added dry and not as a syrup. The hot sugar cooks the egg white before baking, allowing you to bake a meringue that has a lovely soft center.

Ingredients

10½ oz (300 g) superfine
   sugar
5 oz (150 g) (approx. 4) egg
   whites
freeze-dried fruit powder or
   fresh fruit purées,
    to flavor
cocoa powder, to dust

Method

1. Preheat the oven to 400°F (200°C). Put the sugar in a baking dish and cover with foil. Place in the hot oven for 10 to 15 minutes until just beginning to melt around the edges and registering 210°F (100°C) on a thermometer. Remove from the oven and reduce the oven temperature to 210°F (100°C).

2. Place the egg whites in the bowl of a free-standing mixer and start to whisk. Carefully add the hot sugar and whisk until you have a stiff-peaked meringue. Flavor the meringue as you wish. Add a tablespoon (15 g) of freeze-dried fruit powder and ripple through the mix. Fresh fruit purées, rose water and other extracts and essences can also be folded through now.

3. The meringues can be piped (3a) or shaped with a spoon (3b). Once shaped they can be dusted with cocoa or finely chopped nuts. Edible lusters and colored powders can be sifted over just prior to baking.

4. Bake the meringues in the oven at 210°F (100°C) until they are crisp on the outside but soft in the middle. For a 2-inch (5 cm) diameter meringue this will take 20–30 minutes baking. A good test to check the meringue is perfectly cooked is to measure the internal temperature with a digital thermometer. A meringue with an internal temperature of 160°F (72°C) when it leaves the oven will cool to a meringue that's soft on the inside.

3a

3b

4

CANELÉS

It's a little difficult to understand exactly what happens to a canelé batter in the oven. The pastry gods transform the vanilla- and rum-flavored mix into a crisp caramelized shell containing a moist set custard. They are at their best for about 4 hours after baking, but the batter must be made the day before to allow excess air to escape, or during baking they will erupt all over your oven. You'll need canelé molds, too.

Ingredients

1²/₅ cups (340 ml) milk

¾ oz (20 g) butter

1 vanilla pod, split and seeds removed

2½ oz (70 g) all-purpose flour

2 eggs

½ tsp (2.5 g) salt

4½ oz (125 g) superfine sugar

¹/₅ cup (50 ml) good dark rum

Method

1. Warm the milk in a pot with the butter, vanilla pod and seeds until the butter melts. Remove from the heat and set aside to allow the vanilla flavors to infuse.

2. Sift the flour into a bowl and whisk in the whole eggs followed by the sugar then the milk, butter and vanilla mix. Fish out the vanilla pod to whisk in the milk but return to the mix afterwards. Pour in the rum. Ensure the mix is well combined, then cover the bowl and refrigerate overnight.

3. Preheat the oven to 400°F (200°C). Remove the vanilla pod and stir the mix gently as it may have separated a little overnight. Place the molds on a baking tray and fill with batter to about ½ inch (1 cm) from the top of the mold. Place in the oven for 20 minutes, then turn the heat down to 350°F (180°C) and bake for up to a further 40 minutes. The finished canelés should be a dark brown, almost burned color. Allow them to cool to room temperature but then eat them quickly.

LANGUES DE CHAT

These are small, crisp cookies shaped like a cat's tongue. They can be partially dipped in chocolate or flavored with citrus zest.

Make sure the butter is soft. This is a mix that is piped and it will be impossible to do so if the butter is hard.

Ingredients

4½ oz (125 g) butter

4½ oz (125 g) confectioners' sugar

2½ oz (75 g) (approx. 2) egg white

½ tsp (2.5 ml) vanilla extract

5½ oz (160 g) all-purpose flour

Method

1. Cream the butter and confectioners' sugar together until pale and fluffy. Gradually add the egg whites until you have a smooth homogenous mix. Add the vanilla, then gently fold in the flour but be careful not to over-work the mix.

2. Preheat the oven to 335°F (170°C). Fit a piping bag with a ¼-inch (5 mm) plain round nozzle and fill the bag with the mix. Line a baking sheet with silicone paper or a silicone mat. Pipe 4-inch (10 cm) long strips onto the tray, leaving 1½ inches (4 cm) between each strip as the batter will spread.

3. Bake in the oven for 9 to 11 minutes or until the edges are browned but the center of the cookie remains pale.

Variations

Instead of vanilla, the zest of a lemon or orange may be added. After baking and cooling, the cookies may be dipped in chocolate.

PÂTES AUX FRAISES [STRAWBERRY JELLIES]

Perhaps not quite a cake, these are certainly a classic petit four. High-quality fruit purées are widely available and allow the creation of fresh and interesting jellies. The trick to making a good jelly is to keep them uncomplicated and perfectly set. Pectin works best here as it gives a denser textured jelly, though it can be a little temperamental to use.

Ingredients

0.35 oz (10 g) yellow (HM) pectin

16 oz (450 g) superfine sugar, plus extra for coating

1³/₅ cups (400 ml) strawberry purée

1½ oz (40 g) glucose

¼ oz (5 g) citric acid dissolved in 1 tsp (5 ml) water

flavorless vegetable oil

Method

1. Prepare a frame or mold for the jellies. The above quantities will fill an 8 x 8-inch (20 x 20 cm) square tray to a depth of approximately ½ inch (1 cm). Line the tray with plastic wrap.

2. Mix the pectin with 3½ oz (100 g) of the superfine sugar. Place the purée in a pot and whisk in the sugar and pectin mix. Heat the purée and bring to the boil. Add the remaining sugar and glucose to the pot and continue to heat to 224°F (107°C), checking the temperature constantly. At that point remove from the heat and quickly stir in the citric acid. Pour the hot mix into the tray.

3. Leave the jellies to set overnight. Remove from the tray and cut them into even shapes. Lightly coat the pieces with oil to seal them and prevent them from going sticky during storage. Then toss the pieces in a bowl of superfine sugar to coat evenly. Once oiled and sugared the pâte de fruit pieces will keep for at least one month.

FILLINGS
... &FROSTINGS

If pastry cases, macaron shells and sponges are the sensible members of the patisserie family, fillings and frostings are their naughty cousins. There is perhaps a little less vital technique involved in making them and a little bit of fun to be had. Modern cooking processes and the availability of new ingredients and flavors allow for an infinite range of fillings and frostings, but the classic creams, ganaches and jellies should be your starting point.

The techniques associated with molecular gastronomy are increasingly used in modern patisserie. They create extraordinary textures and tastes, but when you're feeling hungry, a cake filled with vanilla-scented crème pâtissière can't be beaten.

How to Make
CRÈME PÂTISSIÈRE

Crème pâtissière is the starting point for a number of other fillings. In almost all recipes it's best to make your crème pâtissière in advance and allow it to cool completely and preferably overnight in a refrigerator. If you can, use fresh vanilla pods; a fresh Tahitian vanilla pod would be ideal.

Ingredients

2¼ oz (60 g) (approx. 3) egg yolks
2¼ oz (60 g) superfine sugar
1 oz (25 g) all-purpose flour
1 vanilla pod
1 cup (250 ml) milk

Tools

Large mixing bowl
Whisk
Small knife
Small pot
Spatula

Method

Step 1

Place the egg yolks and sugar in a bowl and whisk together until well combined. Add the flour and whisk until you have a thick yellow paste.

Step 2

Split the vanilla pod with a small knife and scrape out the seeds. Place the milk, seeds and split vanilla pod in a small pot and heat until it just starts to boil.

Step 3

Remove the vanilla pod from the hot milk and then pour the milk onto the eggs, sugar and flour, whisking continuously. When it's well combined, return to a clean pot. Don't return it to the pot you've just heated the milk in as almost certainly the milk will have burned a little on the base of the pot which will taint the texture or cause lumps to form. Cook on a moderate heat for 2 to 3 minutes until thick.

Fillings & Frostings

112

CRÈME LÉGÈRE

It may seem a little strange to "lighten" crème pâtissière by adding cream, but folding in softly whipped cream lightens both the texture and taste. Crème légère can be used in the same way as crème pâtissière, and works well with fresh summer berries and lighter cakes.

Ingredients

1 quantity crème pâtissière
   (see page 112), cooled
¾ cup (180 ml) heavy cream

Method

Briefly whisk the crème pâtissière to revive it. Whisk the cream to soft peaks and gently fold into the crème pâtissière.

CRÈME MOUSSELINE

As with crème légère, the consistency of the crème pâtissière is lightened with butter. Use unsalted butter as it will be apparent if you don't. Crème mousseline is used in the classic Gâteau Fraisier to sandwich rounds of genoise sponge and fresh strawberries.

Ingredients

1 quantity of crème pâtissière
   (see page 112), cooled
8 oz (225 g) unsalted butter,
   at room temperature

Method

Briefly whisk the crème pâtissière to revive it and then whisk in the softened butter. The butter needs to be really soft to emulsify with the crème or you will be left with large lumps of unincorporated butter.

Fillings & Frostings

CRÈME CHIBOUST

Crème Chiboust is best known for its part in a Gâteau Saint-Honoré, where crème pâtissière is combined with Italian meringue and used to the fill choux buns that decorate the gâteau. Classically it is piped using a v-shaped nozzle. It must be made and eaten the same day.

Ingredients

1 quantity of crème pâtissière (see page 112), at room temperature
10½ oz (300 g) superfine sugar
⅓ cup (80 ml) water
3½ oz (100 g) egg white

Method

1. Heat the sugar and water in a small pot until it reaches 242°F (117°C). As the temperature gets close to 242°F (117°C), start to whisk the egg whites in the bowl of a free-standing mixer until a little frothy. When at the correct temperature, pour the syrup in a thin stream onto the eggs and continue to whisk until you have stiff peaks and the meringue is cool.

2. Whisk the crème pâtissière briefly to revive it and then fold the meringue in gently.

How to Make
CRÈME CHANTILLY

This works best with a high fat cream such as whipping or heavy cream.
Whipping cream (fat content 35 percent) is best as it has
enough fat in it to stabilize itself once piped, but is lighter in taste
than a chantilly made from double cream (fat content 48 percent).

The cream must be refrigerator-cold, and if possible the bowl and whisk
should be just as cold.

Ingredients

⅕ cup (200 ml) whipping
cream

1 oz (25 g) confectioners'
sugar

Method

Place the cream in a bowl that is small enough to give a good depth of cream
to whisk. Whisk until almost at the soft peak stage and then add the sugar.
Continue to whisk until light, fluffy and holds a soft peak.

Flavoring Cream

Cream is best when simply flavored. Quick variants include adding
vanilla as either seeds or extract. A small amount of rose water works
beautifully in cream particularly when paired with fresh raspberries.
Similarly, a small amount of fresh fruit purée, or at Christmas a
sweetened chestnut purée, can give an elegant finish when rippled
through cream.

Small amounts of your favorite spirit can also be added to crème
chantilly at the point at which you add the sugar: rum and
Cointreau work particularly well.

How to Make
CHOCOLATE GANACHE

Depending on the role it will take in a cake, a good ganache contains 60 percent white chocolate or 55 percent dark or milk chocolate. The remaining percentage is made up of ingredients that will thin, flavor and stabilize the ganache. These recipes can be easily adapted for your needs.

Ingredients
7 oz (200 g) white chocolate
²/₅ cup (100 ml) heavy cream
1½ oz (40 g) butter, at room
    temperature
    or
7 oz (200 g) dark or milk chocolate
¼ cup (125 ml) heavy cream
1½ oz (40 g) butter, at room
    temperature

Tools
Food processor
Medium-sized pot
Spatula
Hand-held blender
Whisk

Method

Step 1
Chop the chocolate finely in a food processor. Be warned: it will be noisy!

Step 2
Heat the cream in the pot until almost boiling. Pour over the chocolate in a bowl. After 30 seconds, stir with a spatula until smooth. Use a hand-held blender on lumps of unmelted chocolate.

Step 3
Wait until the ganache has cooled to room temperature and whisk to incorporate the butter.

Infusing Flavor
Cream can be infused with a variety of flavors before emulsifying with the chocolate. White chocolate works well with coffee, tea, vanilla, coconut and lemon. Try nuts, mint, spices and caramel with milk and dark chocolate.

Fruit Purées
Replacing cream with fruit purée works to lighten a ganache. The viscosity of the purée alters the amount of chocolate required. For a thick apple or blackcurrant purée reduce the chocolate to as low as 50 per cent. A thin passion fruit purée works with at least 60 per cent chocolate.

Chocolate and Water Ganache
Going against everything once taught about cooking with chocolate, French chemist Hervé This invented a new way of combining water and chocolate (see page 120) through molecular gastronomy.

Fillings & Frostings

118

BLACKCURRANT
AND WHITE CHOCOLATE GANACHE

Ingredients

7 oz (200 g) white chocolate

⅔ cup (140 ml) blackcurrant
purée

1½ oz (40 g) butter, at room
temperature

Method

Melt the chocolate in a bowl over a pot of simmering water (bain-marie).
Remove the bowl from the heat and whisk in the fruit purée. Allow to cool to
room temperature and then incorporate the butter.

CHOCOLATE AND WATER GANACHE

Ingredients

8 oz (225 g) dark chocolate

⅘ cup (200 ml) water

Method

1. Melt the chocolate and water in a pot. The lecithin present in the
chocolate will help the chocolate and water emulsify. If this fails, a small
amount of gelatin will help the two components come together.

2. Once melted, place the pot in a bowl filled with ice. This will cool the mix
and start to crystallize the chocolate. If you whisk vigorously as the emulsion
cools, air bubbles are introduced which the chocolate will crystallize around.
Once thickened, use in the same way you would a crème chantilly.

PASSION FRUIT AND MILK CHOCOLATE GANACHE

Ingredients

7 oz (200 g) milk chocolate

⅖ cup (100 ml) passion fruit purée

1½ oz (40 g) butter, at room temperature

Method

Melt the chocolate in a bowl over a pot of simmering water (bain-marie). Remove the bowl from the heat and whisk in the fruit purée. Allow to cool to room temperature and then incorporate the butter.

Fillings & Frostings

121

How to Make
BUTTERCREAM

Familiar to most as the topping of the ubiquitous cupcake, buttercream has become a rather clumsy all-purpose cake filling and frosting. There are, however, more refined variants that can flavor, blend and finish patisserie. A good buttercream should be light, silky and well flavored.

Ingredients

3½ oz (100 g) unsalted butter, at
    room temperature
7 oz (200 g) confectioners' sugar
splash of milk

Tools

Large mixing bowl
Hand beater or electric mixer

Method

Beat the butter in a bowl by hand or preferably with a free-standing mixer. Once smooth and fluffy, add a little milk to loosen the mix further. Add the confectioners' sugar and mix until smooth.

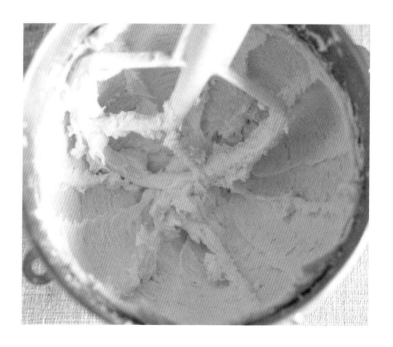

MERINGUE BUTTERCREAM

This buttercream is a rich, sophisticated mix that works especially well when flavored. It's lighter and less sweet than the other buttercreams.

Ingredients

3½ oz (100 g) (approx. 3) egg white

9 oz (250 g) superfine sugar

²/₅ cup (100 ml) water

10½ oz (300 g) unsalted butter, chopped and softened

Method

1. Whisk the egg whites in the bowl of a free-standing mixer at a medium speed. After 30 seconds of whisking, add in 2 oz (50 g) superfine sugar. Continue to whisk until you have soft peaks.

2. Heat the remaining superfine sugar and the water in a small pot until it reaches 242°F (117°C). You need a good depth of liquid to measure the temperature accurately, so if necessary make twice the volume of syrup but only use half. When at temperature pour the syrup onto the meringue mix and start to whisk again. Continue until thick, smooth and cool.

3. Whisk in the butter a little at a time. Make sure the meringue has cooled sufficiently before doing this as if it remains hot it will melt the butter rather than emulsify it. Once thick and cool, flavor as you wish.

Flavoring Buttercreams

Add flavor to your buttercream as the last step. Melted chocolate of all varieties works well, as do essences, extracts and fruit purées. You need to be a careful with alcohol as that can split the emulsion, but go carefully and add small amounts gradually and all will be well.

Fillings & Frostings

123

PÂTE À BOMBE BUTTERCREAM

Incorporating egg yolks into this buttercream produces a rich yellow-tinged frosting and filling. Pâte à bombe is a useful patisserie component and is also used to stabilize and enrich mousses.

Ingredients

4½ oz (125 g) (approx. 6)
  egg yolks

5 oz (140 g) superfine sugar

⅓ cup (80 ml) water

7 oz (200 g) unsalted butter,
  chopped and softened

Method

1. Place the egg yolks in the bowl of a free-standing mixer fitted with a whisk.

2. Combine the sugar and water in a small pot and heat to 242°F (117°C). When at temperature start to whisk the egg yolks and pour the hot sugar syrup in a thin stream onto the eggs. Continue to whisk until pale, thick and cooled.

3. Once cool, add the butter bit by bit. The butter must be soft otherwise it will not emulsify and you'll create lumps.

A wonderful must-try variant of this buttercream uses maple syrup in place of the total weight of sugar and water. Heat it in the same way and make the pâte à bombe. This buttercream is fabulous as a macaron filling, or combined with fresh blueberries as a component in a gâteau.

GELLING AGENTS AND THICKENERS

Gelling agents are used throughout patisserie to stabilize, emulsify and set components. There is an ever-expanding range of gelling agents, from those that don't freeze below 32°F (0°C) to those that won't melt in ovens. One of their best uses is as a means of setting fruit to incorporate bursts of zingy, bright flavor.

● ● ● GELATIN

Gelatin is easy and versatile, but it has its pitfalls. Firstly, don't forget it's an animal product, derived from either pork or beef, so not all are able to eat it.

Gelatin is made in a range of bloom strengths from bronze to platinum. Most but not all suppliers specify that detail on the packaging, and it's important as it will make a significant difference to the amount you need to use. Add gelatin by weight and not by teaspoons of powder or leaves. Leaves vary in size and the teaspoon is an inaccurate measure here. As a guide:

0.42 oz (12 g) of platinum-strength (250 bloom) leaf gelatin will soft-set 4 cups (1,000 ml)
0.7 oz (20 g) of silver-strength (160 bloom) leaf gelatin will soft-set 4 cups (1,000 ml)
1.16 oz (33 g) of bronze-strength (140 bloom) leaf gelatin will soft-set 4 cups (1,000 ml)

● ● ● CARRAGEENAN

Carrageenan is a remarkable gel. Derived from red seaweeds, it has been used for hundreds of years to set desserts, including a traditional Irish blancmange.

There are 3 classes of carrageenan: Kappa, Iota and Lambda. Kappa and Iota gel, Lambda thickens. Kappa produces a brittle gel, Iota makes something softer. Both will set at room temperature and remain set up to 158°F (70°C), allowing for hot jellies.

Carrageenan must be heated to activate it and is used in doses of 0.07–0.35 oz (2–10 g) per 4 cups (1,000 ml).

● ● ● AGAR-AGAR

Derived from a red algae, agar-agar is a mainstay for setting many South-East Asian desserts. One of its major benefits is that it is able to set relatively acidic liquids. Again, it must be heated to activate it.

Try combining 0.07 oz (2 g) of agar-agar with ⅘ cup (200 ml) of passion fruit purée. Whisk together in a pot and heat until it froths. Tip into a small tray or the bottom of a cup and allow to set. Chop into small dice and sprinkle over a chocolate tart to create powerful and lovely bursts of flavor.

••• PECTIN

Extracted from fruit, pectin may be used to set pâte de fruit for petits fours or to thicken fruit-based fillings for macarons and gâteaux.

You need yellow/slow-setting/high-methoxyl (HM) pectin for patisserie work and pectin needs acidity to set properly. The dose required is 1–1.5 percent of the weight of the finished component.

Pectin should be combined with sugar before adding to fruit purées or whatever is being set. It will form lumps if combined on its own. Try to heat the liquid, sugar and pectin mix to the required temperature (222–226°F/106–108°C) quickly as pectin degrades with prolonged heating.

How to Make
FRUIT CURDS

Made well, the buttery tang of fruit curd adds richness and depth to a cake. If made with enough egg yolks, given plenty of fruit juice and chilled well, these curds will cut cleanly in a gâteau or entremet.

The sensible way to cook this curd is in a bowl over a pot of simmering water (a bain-marie), but it's much quicker in a pot over direct heat. As long as you keep whisking and stirring it will work well.

Ingredients

Zest and juice of 4 lemons

12 egg yolks

7 oz (200 g) superfine sugar

7 oz (200 g) butter, melted

Tools

Small pot

Spatula

Large mixing bowl

Whisk

Sieve

Variations

To make lime or passion fruit curd, use 6 limes or $2/3$ cup (160 ml) passion fruit purée in place of the lemons and proceed with the rest of the recipe.

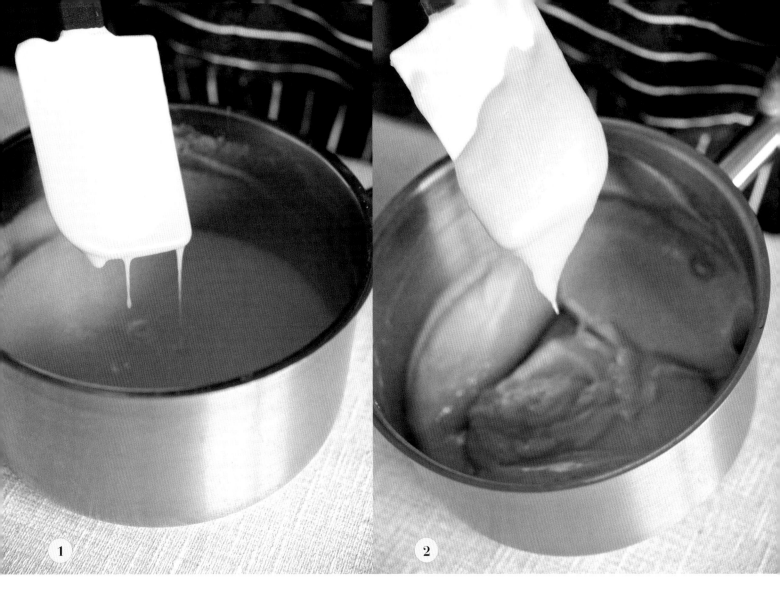

1

2

Method

Step 1
Combine the lemon juice and zest with a spatula in a small pot and heat until the juice has reduced by half. The mixture will not be especially thick yet.

Step 2
Combine the egg yolks, sugar and melted butter in a bowl with a whisk. Pass the reduced juice through a small sieve into the mix and warm gently. You'll need a whisk to keep things smooth and a spatula to stop the curd from sticking to the edges. Warm gently until transformed from a thin glossy mix to a thick cream.

How to Make
GLAZES

A good glaze will take your cake from kitchen table to Parisian patisserie window. They are incredibly effective at creating uniformity of design and appearance (and will also cover a multitude of sins).

The key technique here is getting the temperature of the uncovered cake and the temperature of the glaze correct.

CLEAR GLAZES

This is effectively a clear, flavorless jelly. It can be varied to create a fruit glaze by replacing half the water with fruit purée.

Ingredients

0.35 oz (10 g) yellow pectin

7½ oz (210 g) superfine sugar

⁴⁄₅ cup (200 ml) water

1 tsp (16 ml) liquid glucose

Method

Step 1

Mix the pectin with 2 oz (50 g) of the superfine sugar. Heat the water to 140°F (60°C) and then whisk in the pectin and another 2 oz (50 g) of sugar. Bring to a boil and then whisk in the remaining sugar. Bring back to a boil and add the liquid glucose.

Step 2

Remove from the heat and allow to cool completely, preferably overnight. Before applying, it needs to be re-heated to 95°F (35°C) in a small bowl over simmering water (bain-marie). At 95°F (35°C) the glaze can be poured or brushed over the cake or gâteau.

CHOCOLATE GLAZES

This glaze gives such an elegant and refined finish. A cake completely covered in it or in opulent gold leaf looks stunning.

Ingredients

¹/₃ cup (80 ml) water

7 oz (200 g) superfine sugar

²/₃ cup (160 ml) heavy cream

¹/₃ cup (80 ml) liquid glucose

4 tbsp (60 g) cocoa powder

0.42 oz (12 g) silver leaf gelatin,
   softened in cold water

Method

Step 1

Place the water, sugar, cream and glucose in a small pot and whisk together. Place over a moderate heat and add the cocoa powder. Bring to a boil. Remove from the heat and allow to cool.

Step 2

Once cooled to 140°F (60°C), add the softened gelatin, then allow to cool completely. To use, re-heat to 95°F (35°C).

Step 3

To glaze the cake, place it on a wire rack over a tray and pour the glaze over. You need to cover the cake quickly and ideally with one application of glaze, otherwise you won't achieve a flat, even surface. Small irregularities in the glaze can be cleverly rectified by re-heating it with a hairdryer. Use the dryer on its lowest setting and gently waft over the surface of the cake; the ripples will slowly melt away. Be careful with this technique, however, as it is easy to melt any mousse or ganache layer underneath the glaze.

CRÈMES MISTAKES

There are a few things that can go wrong with crèmes and ganaches but with a little practice these are easily remedied. Firstly, find out what went wrong and compare your results with the pictures below.

● ● ● CRÈME PÂTISSIÈRE

THIN AND RUNNY

The crème pâtissière needs to be cooked adequately on the stove for the egg and flour to thicken the milk. A common mistake is to assume that cooling and refrigeration of the crème pâtissière will thicken it. That's correct, but you need to start with a crème with a thick consistency before cooling.

LUMPY

Cook the crème slowly and pay attention to the sides of the pot. You may require a whisk to keep the consistency smooth and a spatula to reach the corners of the pot.

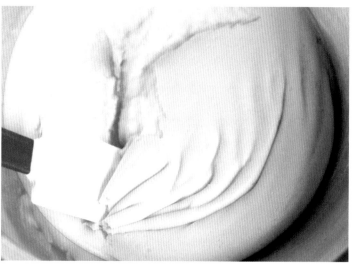

SKIN FORMATION

Once cooked, the crème will naturally form a skin. This can be easily prevented by pressing plastic wrap onto the surface of the crème itself and then refrigerating.

• • • FRESH CREAM

OVER-WHIPPED

A free-standing mixer makes light work of whisking cream, but it's easy to over-whip it and cause the cream to become grainy. If using a mixer, stand over it and watch it all the time. Stop whisking before you need to and finish the job by hand.

If the cream is to be piped, it's best to slightly under-whip it. The process of filling a piping bag and piping it through a nozzle affects the texture of the cream, almost whipping it further as you pipe.

• • • GANACHE

SPLIT GANACHE

A chocolate ganache is an emulsion of fat (cocoa butter/fat from cream and/or butter) and water (from the cream/purée). A split ganache occurs if there is too much fat in the mix, or if the mix is stirred while the fat droplets are crystallizing.

Don't despair if this happens, as the ganache can almost always be saved. In the first instance, re-heat the ganache to release the fat and allow it to crystallize correctly. If that doesn't work then add a little more moisture: don't use cream as this contains too much fat, but alcohol, milk or water will work.

DECORATING
... &PRESENTING

This aspect of patisserie could be viewed as the tricky bit, the final complex detail that is unachievable without years of experience. But this is not necessarily so. Decorating is not hard, so grab your piping bag and paint brushes — you can do it!

Admittedly, watching a patisserie grand master pull hot sugar or shape molten chocolate is a feat to be marveled at, but the real elegance and beauty comes from a cake that is brilliantly made and simply finished. Play to your strengths and with what tools you have available. If you're an experienced cake decorator, pipe a final frosting detail. If you have a garden, adorn the cake with edible petals. If it's in season, use your favorite fresh fruit. Have fun with it.

How to Make
FONDANT FROSTING

Used sparingly, rolled fondant frosting can add useful design details to large and small cakes. Roll it thin and keep it to a minimum; acres of thick, sugary fondant don't add much to refined patisserie other than impenetrable sweetness. Making fondant at home is possible and interesting to do, but there is no perceivable difference between home-made and store-bought. Sugar is sugar, so buy it ready-made.

Ingredients
Ready-made or store-bought
    fondant frosting
Confectioners' sugar for dusting

Tools
Rolling pin

WORKING WITH FONDANT FROSTING
You'll need to knead the fondant into a workable consistency. Dust the work surface and the rolling pin with confectioners' sugar. Lift and move the fondant as you work to prevent it from sticking.

How to Make
ROYAL ICING

Royal icing is the perfect component to add detail and finesse to your creations. It's barely a recipe, just a simple mix of confectioners' sugar, egg white and a little lemon juice. The quantities below should be seen as a starting point. For small piped detail work you may need a thicker mix, so add less egg white; for covering larger areas of cake with smooth, flat icing you may need to add a little more egg white.

Ingredients
2½ oz (75 g) (approx. 2) egg white
14 oz (400 g) confectioners' sugar
2 tsp (10 ml) lemon juice

Tools
Large mixing bowl
Whisk
Sieve
Large mixing spoon

Method
Whisk the egg whites until frothy then sift the confectioners' sugar on top and stir to combine. Stir in the lemon juice.

Helpful Hint
If you want to cover an 8-inch cake with royal icing, double the quantities of ingredients. To cover and decorate the cake, you'll need to triple them.

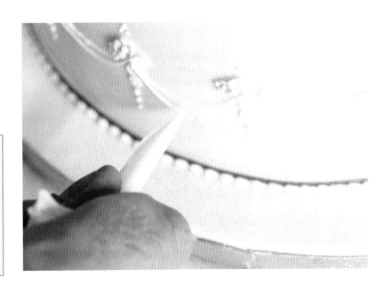

Decorating & Presenting

137

PIPING SKILLS

Piping is about having the right nozzle, the right consistency of frosting, and confidence. Practice off the cake before trying it for real. With royal icing, the detailing can be piped onto an acetate sheet and transferred when dry. Mark out the icing details with pin pricks on the cake before piping.

••• NOZZLES

There are only a few nozzles that you will use over and over again — you don't need a set with 30 different types as they won't get used. A selection of plain and star-shaped nozzles is enough to start with, and as you become more experienced you may wish to add in nozzles for particular tasks: for example, a v-shaped nozzle for piping Chiboust cream (see page 114), or a larger fluted nozzle to pipe éclairs (see page 39).

••• PIPING BAGS

Disposable piping bags (see Resources, page 156) are more practical than reusable cloth bags. A reusable bag can only be cut to one size, and if used infrequently they sit in the back of your kitchen drawer gathering dust and mold.

Knowing how to make your own piping bag out of silicone paper is a useful skill, particularly when you only need to pipe a small amount.

Making a Piping Bag

Step 1
Cut an oblong sheet of greaseproof paper. Fold the end of the paper to form a right-angled triangle.

Step 2
Cut the triangle from the sheet.

Step 3
With the long tip of the triangle in front of you, roll the right-hand corner round to form a cone. The right-hand corner will meet the center point of the triangle.

Step 4
Wrap around the left-hand corner of the triangle to meet the center point.

Step 5
Evenly line up all the corners to form the final cone.

Step 6
Fold over the top of the cone to fix and secure the cone shape.

Step 7
Fill the cone with a mixture. Fold down the top of the cone (see page 138, left), attach the nozzle and use.

CHOCOLATE

With a bit of practice and an understanding of the science behind it,
chocolate is a quick and easy way to decorate a cake.

••• CHOCOLATE EQUIPMENT

A few select pieces of equipment will help with chocolate work. A piece of marble or granite work surface will help cool the chocolate and provide a flat, crack-free surface on which to create chocolate shapes and decorations.

An offset spatula is essential to create a smooth, flat surface of chocolate, while a selection of small and large scrapers are invaluable when creating curls and ruffles. Scrapers are also important when you are cleaning up as they will do a quick job of removing chocolate from your work surface. Buy them from your local DIY store rather than pastry or chocolatier suppliers — they will be much cheaper.

{1} FLEXIBLE SCRAPER
Perfect for working chocolate on a tempering stone. This tool is also perfect for cutting and chopping chocolate, dough and icing.

{2, 3, 4} DIPPING FORKS
Designed for dipping fruit, truffles and other small items into melted chocolate. They can also be used to create decorative touches.

{5} DECORATING COMB
The serrated sides enable you to make lines, patterns and textures on icing, pastries and chocolate. You can also create chocolate straws and decorative feathering.

{6} SMALL HANDLED SCRAPER
Used like a flexible scraper, this is shaped to give you greater ease of use. The handle of this scraper is at a perpendicular angle to the blade.

{7} LARGE HANDLED SCRAPER
With a larger blade than its small cousin's, this scraper allows you to do everything including making chocolate curls.

{8} SMALL OFFSET SPATULA
This tool is excellent for cleaning chocolate molds and to smooth across filled chocolate molds for a clean finish.

{9} SPATULA
It lacks the angled blade of offset spatulas but is just as useful for spreading fillings and smoothing soft surfaces.

{10} LARGE OFFSET SPATULA
With this large blade you can smooth chocolate across flat surfaces, even out icing and frosting, and spread caramel.

••• DECORATIONS

Chocolate may be piped into small designs or spread into thin sheets and then cut or broken into shards or shaped into curls and ruffles.

The starting point for these decorations is a thin layer of tempered chocolate. The chocolate needs to set a little before working. Once the glossy liquid surface has become matte and dulled the chocolate can be cut into shapes. Using a scraper, the chocolate can be lifted in strips to form 2½–3½-inch (6–8 cm) wide ruffles.

To create small curls to decorate the sides of gâteaux, a thin layer of chocolate is prepared in the same way, but after spreading it is immediately re-spread with a serrated cake comb. This creates multiple thin lines of chocolate. Allow to harden slightly then scrape off small strips to create the curls.

PLAQUES AND SMEARS
1. Small chocolate plaques and smears can be placed around the edge of a gateau to give a clean and elegant finish. Cut precisely and carefully placed, they give the impression of extraordinary complexity when the cake within is actually deceptively simple.

RUFFLES AND CURLS
2. Ruffles and curls can again edge a gâteau but similarly look dramatic and add height, when piled on top of small and larger cakes. The way chocolate bends and folds gives intriguing visual detail.

SWIRLS AND SCRIBBLES
3. Small swirls and chaotic scribbles contrast well when used to decorate simple plain patisserie. They need a plain surface to sit on, like a white wall covered in chocolate graffiti.

••• ACETATE

As with lining cake frames for gâteaux, acetate gives an amazing finish to chocolate. Simple plaques and tiles to cover your cakes can be made using tempered chocolate spread thinly on an acetate sheet. Once on the sheet the chocolate can be molded further by covering it with a second sheet and rolling it up, creating curves.

Complete chocolate surrounds for gâteaux and smaller cakes can also be made this way. Cut a strip of acetate to the dimensions of the side of your cake. Spread a thin layer of tempered chocolate on the acetate. Allow to cool briefly but not completely, then wrap the strip around the cake and leave to set hard.

USING COCOA BUTTER TRANSFERS

These come as transfers printed on a sheet of acetate. Use them in the same way you would acetate by spreading tempered chocolate on them and allowing to set. As the chocolate crystallizes, the cocoa butter is transferred to the surface of the chocolate.

SPRAYING WITH CHOCOLATE

If you're considering trying this you may wish to build a small extension that can be used for this purpose alone! Chocolate gets absolutely everywhere. You have been warned. But although messy, it does give an amazing, almost velvety finish to a cake.

Cover the cake with an even and smooth layer of ganache or mousse and freeze it. Fill a spray gun — a cheap domestic spray gun works fine — with a 50/50 mix of melted cocoa butter and whatever chocolate you want to use, again melted and mixed with the liquid cocoa butter. Place the frozen cake on a stand and spray with a thin, even coat from 2–3 feet (60–90 cm) away. If doing this inside you'll need to spray the cake in a contained space such as a large box or container. Don't just spray it on your work surface.

How to
TEMPER CHOCOLATE

Chocolate is a mix of cocoa solids, cocoa butter, sugar and milk solids. In order for chocolate to have its shiny surface and the characteristic snap on breaking, the cocoa butter needs to be crystallized. If you simply melt chocolate and allow it to re-set, the wrong sort of cocoa butter fat crystals form. These crystals are unstable and give the chocolate a dull finish, no snap and a poor texture when eaten. So when you melt chocolate to shape it into your chosen decoration, you need to re-create these stable fat crystals.

Ingredients
Chocolate bars, pieces or chips

Tools
Bain-marie or metal bowl and pot

Large spatula or wooden spoon

Microwave-safe bowl

Hand-held blender

Keeping the chocolate in temper
Once melted and in temper the chocolate may be held until ready to use by placing it in a bowl over a pot of hot water (bain-marie). The ideal working temperatures at which to hold the chocolate are:

Dark: 90°F (32°C)

Milk: 86°F (30°C)

White: 82°F (28°C)

Seeding

Both of the methods described involve 'seeding' the melted chocolate with tempered chocolate, setting off a chain reaction that encourages stable fat crystals to form. Neither method is as reliable as more complex tabling techniques, but for the purposes of cake decoration, and with the relatively small quantities of chocolate involved, they are good enough.

Method 1

Divide the amount of chocolate you want to melt into thirds (1). Warm two-thirds of the chocolate in a bowl over simmering water (bain-marie) until just melted (2). Now add the unmelted, and still in temper, chocolate into the melted chocolate and stir until all the chocolate is melted (3). If unmelted lumps of chocolate remain, these can be fished out before using. Check that the chocolate is in temper (see page 144) and use.

Method 2

Place all the chocolate in a microwave-safe bowl and microwave on a moderate setting in 10-second bursts. After each 10 seconds remove the chocolate and stir. Repeat this process until the chocolate begins to melt. You do not want to melt the chocolate completely, only partially. You need a final mix of lumps of unmelted chocolate suspended in melted liquid chocolate.

Now stick blend until smooth (4). At this point the unmelted lumps of chocolate (still in temper) will be dispersed and seed the chocolate with the correct fat crystals.

SUGAR

Sugar adds sparkle and light to patisserie: natural sunlight glinting on sugarwork gives the illusion of cake jewelry. Sugarwork is also a clever way of adding crunch and texture.

• • • ISOMALT

Isomalt is a sugar that melts to a clear transparent finish. Simply sprinkle it on a silicone mat and bake in a moderate oven (325°F/160°C) until it melts. When cooled it sets into a clear sugar window. Colorings in the form of powders or sprinkles can be baked into the isomalt to add interest. Isomalt sugar is less hygroscopic, and decorations made from it will hold up better.

  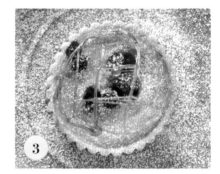

• • • CARAMEL

Making and working with caramel is quick and great fun. It's something to practice on a wet afternoon.

To make the caramel, place superfine sugar in a dry pot and heat (1). Note that when you are heating sugar by itself, i.e., without water, it is necessary to stir the sugar to help it melt evenly. Do not leave it unattended as the caramel will burn quickly. Heat the pot until all the sugar has melted (2) into a soft, light brown color.

The sugar will continue to cook from the residual heat in the pot, so it needs to be cooled. Place the bottom of the pot in a bowl of water. This will create lots of steam so be careful not to be looking into the pot when doing so.

For making caramel shards, the sugar should be poured out and spread thinly onto a silicone mat or lightly oiled sheet of foil. Allow it to set and cool, then snap into glass-like slivers of sugar.

For spun sugar (3) and spirals you need the caramel to cool and thicken slightly.

When making spun sugar, the caramel needs to cling to a small spoon or a fork. The spoon is then held over a sharpening steel and flicked back and forth. It is propelled over the spoon in fine threads and gathers over the steel.

Before the sugar sets, the fine sugar strands can be molded into a cloud to be placed on the cake.

In making spirals of sugar the caramel is delicately wrapped around the sharpening steel.

••• NOUGATINE

Nougatine starts as an almond brittle. Toasted flaked almonds are added to caramel and spread thinly on a silicone mat to set. Once cooled, the brittle is blitzed in a food processor to a fine dust.

The almond sugar dust is then sifted onto a silicone mat to a depth of around $1/16$–$1/8$ inch (1–2 mm) before being re-melted in the oven. Be careful if you have a fan-assisted oven — you may need to turn the fan off as the sugar will be blown around the oven and be rather difficult to clean.

Once the sugar has re-melted and is an even brown color, the nougatine is ready. Remove from the oven and cut into the shapes required (see photo: middle row left). If the nougatine is to be molded it may need to be initially cut to shape and then re-heated briefly in the oven, removed and then molded.

••• BRITTLES

Adding nuts to caramelized sugar creates a quick nut brittle. Pour onto a silicone mat and spread thinly. Brittles can be used in big pieces to add height and drama, or crumbled into small chunks to create a crisp decorative finish (see photo: bottom row, right).

••• ANATOMY OF SUGAR

To work with sugar it needs to be heated to high temperatures. Be careful: molten sugar is hot and sticky. It's easy to burn yourself. Prepare all that you'll need in advance and think through the steps required.

Sugar is also hygroscopic (water-loving), and after you've created your sugar delights they will naturally want to absorb water from the surrounding air. Your creations will become sticky within 20 to 30 minutes. Make decorations just before serving or store them in an airtight container with silica gel sachets.

FRESH FRUIT & FLOWERS

Allowing mother nature to do the hard work for you is an understated and elegant way of decorating. But as with everything, there are a few points to bear in mind when selecting your decorations.

• • • ADVICE

FRESH FRUIT
Make sure the fruit used is perfectly ripe and in season. The generic strawberry decoration is only acceptable in summer, and on patisserie that matches its flavor.

FLOWERS
Care must be taken when using flowers. You need to establish that the flower is edible and that you have identified it correctly.

PETALS
Fresh and candied petals can be used, including roses, violets and pot marigolds.

LUSTERS, SPRINKLES, GOLD & OTHER MAGIC

A kaleidoscope of patisserie finishes are available: sparkly edible glitters, metallic lusters and sugar diamonds. Used judiciously they can work well, but don't let them become the focus of the cake and only use one at a time. No one wants to eat a cake that looks like a tie-dyed T-shirt.

• • • TYPES OF FINISHES

GOLD LEAF
A particularly brilliant finish is a small amount of gold leaf. Yes it's expensive, but you'll only need a small amount. The 'Is that real gold?' reaction heightens expectations and appetites.

LUSTERS
Edible lusters are available in a range of shades and colors. These can be bought as fine powders or sprays and can be applied to finished cakes or their decorations to add glamorous shine and shimmer.

SPRINKLES
Both artificial and natural substances can be lightly sprinkled on cakes. Finely chopped teas, nuts and dried fruit add a simple finish. More exotic sugar diamonds, edible glitters and crystals can add a touch of bling to your creations.

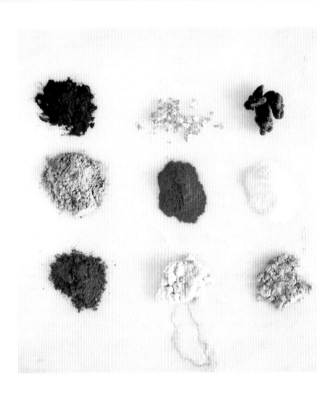

OTHER FINISHES
Sugar 'tattoos' can be bought in a range of designs and applied to chocolate work or direct to cakes. Printed marshmallow designs offer an unusual and striking finish. As with all cake decorations, don't allow these flourishes and final touches to dominate your design. Use them sparingly.

DECORATING & PRESENTING MISTAKES

Presentation comes with its own set of difficulties. Luckily, these are easily spotted and whether you remedy them or have to start over, you'll be getting closer to your perfect patisserie skills.

••• CHOCOLATE

IS IT TEMPERED?

Tempered chocolate sets quickly and without any visible streaks. Take a small amount and drizzle it on the work surface. It should set hard with a shiny finish. If it doesn't, re-heat the chocolate and re-seed with more tempered chocolate.

BLOOM

Bloom is the gray streaks or spots that appear on the surface of chocolate and is caused by either fat or sugar. Fat bloom appears quickly in incorrectly tempered chocolate. Sugar bloom appears later and as a consequence of the chocolate being exposed to moisture or humidity. Both have a similar appearance, but it's possible to differentiate between the two by rubbing your finger on the surface of the chocolate. Sugar bloom feels rough, fat bloom feels smooth.

10 TIPS FOR PERFECTING YOUR PATISSERIE

RELAX
The detail and technique involved in perfecting patisserie requires clear, free-flowing thought. An agitated or uptight mood will lead to imperfect, grumpy cakes. Pause, relax and bake gracefully, focusing on the work.

USE THE BEST POSSIBLE INGREDIENTS
Buy the best quality ingredients. It makes a difference. From exotic flavors to perfectly ripe fruit, patisserie is only as tasty as its components.

TASTE EVERYTHING
Perfect patisserie isn't achieved by carefully constructing a beautiful cake and standing back with fingers crossed, hoping it will taste as good as it looks. Taste the different parts as you make them, amending as necessary. Add more sugar or fruit, or bake a little longer or shorter to refine your work.

CUT BAKING TIMES
One of the most common baking errors is to over-bake. Cakes, biscuits, macarons — almost the full range of baked cakes — will continue to cook once removed from the oven. Try removing them a little earlier from the oven if you find the results have been a bit dry or tough.

GET REALLY GOOD AT MAKING ONE CAKE
Some of the recipes in this book are a little fiddly and may require practice. It's worthwhile repeating some of them and getting really good at one or two. The principles and skills you'll learn in refining your techniques will assist your baking and patisserie as a whole.

CLEAN UP AS YOU GO ALONG
As well as the health benefits of having a clean kitchen, a tidy and well-ordered work space translates into a clean and ordered frame of mind. That frame of mind produces clever, pretty and precise patisserie.

ALLOW ENOUGH TIME
Once practiced, you'll whizz through these recipes at lightning speed and with a flourish. However, some of the recipes may be unfamiliar to start with. Give yourself time to get to know the techniques and methods. Almost all of the more complex cakes can be made in stages that can be spread over a day or two. Take your time and enjoy yourself.

BUILD CAKES SLOWLY
This tip is closely related to the one preceding it, but the difference is important. Many of the cakes in this book can be made in short spells over a few days. The principle of working carefully applies throughout patisserie, and finished cakes are often better for their gradual construction. This allows components to settle, cool and mature. An éclair iced two days ago and filled with a crème pâtissière chilled overnight in a choux bun made that morning, will be much easier to finish than a version constructed under pressure in a hour or two.

INEXPENSIVE EQUIPMENT
Spend money on the bits of equipment you'll use every time you bake and on those that make the biggest difference to the work. Frankly, a bowl is a bowl. A cheaper supermarket version will do the job just as well as its expensive stainless steel cousin. However, an accurate set of digital scales able to measure in 0.5 g increments will outperform an analogue version, and you'll make better cakes using it. Free-standing mixers, good knives and thermometers cost a bit of money. Bowls and spatulas shouldn't.

KEEP IT SIMPLE
Getting better at baking doesn't mean making more complex cakes. It's an easy trap to fall into when you want to challenge yourself. Improving your patisserie skills is as much about perfecting a component and baking a cake consistently well as it is about ticking off the latest recipe or unusual technique. People will remember your perfect macaron, but they are less likely to recall your molecular gastronomy-inspired-upside-down-17-flavors-of-strawberry-spherified-meringue. Well, they might remember it, but probably for the wrong reasons.

GLOSSARY

ACETATE
A flexible plastic used to create a
smooth shiny surface on cakes and
chocolate.

BAIN-MARIE
A heat proof bowl placed over a pan
of simmering water. Used to gently
warm or melt pâtisserie components
such as chocolate, curds, custards and
pâtisserie fondant.

BEURRE NOISETTE
A burned butter created by heating
butter in a small pan until the milk
solids brown and give the butter a
richy nutty flavor.

BLIND BAKE
The baking of a pastry case without
its final contents. The pastry is
weighted down in the oven to give
an even bake and to prevent it rising.

CARAMEL
Molten sugar created by the heating
of dry sugar in a pan or with the
addition of a small amount of water.
Different degrees of caramelization
giving different flavors. A blonde
pale subtle sugar taste to a rich dark
almost burned taste.

CRÈME CHANTILLY
Whipped and sweetened cream
that may be flavored.

CRÈME CHIBOUST
Crème pâtissière combined
with Italian meringue.

CRÈME LÉGÈRE
Crème pâtissière lightened
with double cream.

CRÈME MOUSSELINE
Crème pâtissière combined
with softened butter.

CRÈME PÂTISSIÈRE
The classic pâtisserie filling. A cooked
custard thickened with eggs and flour/
cornflour.

DACQUOISE
A meringue with the addition of
ground almonds and then baked
in thin sheets or discs.

FONDANT
The combination of sugar, glucose,
water and sometimes gelatin can
create a range of different textures
and solid states:

Pâtisserie fondant
This may be poured and is bought as a semi solid lump to be reheated and used to glaze pâtisserie such as éclairs and other choux pastry.

Roll Out / Cake Covering Fondant
Supplied as a more solid block and rolled out like pastry to cover firmer cakes and gâteaux.

GANACHE
An emulsion of chocolate and liquid. The liquid is usually cream or fruit purée.

GÉNOISE
The workhorse of the pastry kitchen. A light an airy sponge made with whole eggs. The rise of the sponge is produced by the whisked eggs alone.

JOCONDE
A light sponge flavored and enriched with ground almonds.

MACARON
The best cake. Two almond meringue shells sandwiched together with vibrant and intriguing fillings.

MERINGUE
Whisked egg whites combined with cold (French Meringue) or hot (Italian Meringue) sugar.

MOUSSE
A light and sweetened dessert or pâtisserie component. Aerated with eggs.

NOUGATINE
Sugar caramel combined with nuts and allowed to set. Then blitzed in a food processor and spread in a thin layer to be reheated and shaped.

PÂTE À BOMBE
Whisked egg yolks that are cooked with a hot sugar syrup to create a sweet and light emulsion. Used to stabilize and lighten mousses and creams.

PÂTE À CHOUX
A twice cooked pastry that rises to create hollow cases and shells. The basis of éclairs and cream puffs.

PÂTE SABLÉE
A delicate and sweet pastry that can also be made into small biscuits.

PÂTE SUCRÉE
A sweet buttery and soft pastry used to create tart cases and the bases for small cakes.

TEMPERING (CHOCOLATE)
The process by which chocolate is heated and cooled to create the correct fat structure. Enabling the chocolate to have its characteristic shine and snap.

RESOURCES

THICKENERS, GELLING AGENTS
AND OTHER MOLECULAR
GASTRONOMY EQUIPMENT
WillPowder
www.willpowder.net
866-249-0400

CHOCOLATE &
OTHER PATISSERIE INGREDIENTS
INCLUDING LUSTERS /
SPRAYS / COLORINGS /
FRUIT PURÉES / ICINGS /
COVERINGS / ACETATE SHEETS
Marque Foods
www.marquefoods.com
1-888-992-4114

EQUIPMENT INCLUDING TART
RINGS / SMALL TOOLS /
DESSERT FRAMES / PIPING BAGS
Williams-Sonoma
www.williams-sonoma.com
1-877-812-6235

Kind Arthur Flour
www.kingarthurflour.com
1-800-827-6836

DECORATING
Kitchen Krafts
www.kitchenkrafts.com
800-298-5389

FOOD PROCESSORS
Magimix
www.magimix.com

FREE-STANDING MIXERS
KitchenAid USA
www.kitchenaid.com
1-800-541-6390

PATISSERIE EQUIPMENT
Matfer Bourgeat
www.matferbourgeatusa.com
818-782-0792

SILICON MOLDS AND TRAYS
Sasa Demarle
www.demarleusa.com
609-395-0219

...INDEX